THE CHURCH AND ITS LAITY

Georgia Harkness

THE CHURCH AND ITS LAITY

Abingdon Press
NEW YORK
NASHVILLE

THE CHURCH AND ITS LAITY

Library of Congress Catalog Card Number: 62-8106

B

SET UP, PRINTED, AND BOUND BY THE PARTHENON PRESS, AT NASHVILLE, TENNESSEE, UNITED STATES OF AMERICA

To my students,
both lay and ministerial,
who through the years have taught me much

CONTENTS

INTRODUCTION

AMONG THE MOST IMPORTANT DEVELOPMENTS IN CHRISTIAN LIFE and thought within recent years are a fresh interest in the nature of the Church and concern for the place of the laity within it. These interests, though related, are not identical, and there has been a tendency to pursue each of them without much reference to the other. It is the thesis of this book that they belong together so closely that neither can be examined in its full richness of meaning or made most fruitful in Christian service to the world without clearer understanding of this connection.

But—one may ask—does not everybody know what a church is—an institution to which Christians belong that carries on many religious and social activities? And are not laymen the church members who are not ordained clergymen, ordinary persons whose job it is to pay the preacher and help him run the church? A further reason for writing this book is to challenge the adequacy of these definitions. It will require more than a sentence to say how much more than this a church is or a layman is, but it is hoped that the reader as he proceeds will find a deeper meaning being placed upon both of these familiar terms.

The book is addressed to both clergy and laity, for the conviction that underlies it is that together we make up one Church, with duties and opportunities not so disparate as they are sometimes thought to be. The calling of the Church is one calling—to manifest the Lordship of Christ and the creative, redemptive power of God within the world. There are many channels of service and many means of grace by which this must be done. At the rich diversity of these we must be looking presently. Yet the word spoken of old is still relevant today, "There is one body and one Spirit, just as you were called to the one hope that belongs to your call, one Lord, one faith, one baptism, one God and Father of us all, who is above all and through all and in all." (Eph. 4:4-6.) If the Church today is open to the one Spirit, a fresh baptism of power can come upon it.

For this openness there is today both need and opportunity. Although everywhere in the American scene there is an affluent and engulfing secularism, I do not hold with those who regard this as a "post-Christian" era. There are many faithful Christians in our churches who work devotedly in their activities and in whose personal and even public lives the Christian gospel makes a difference. This needs to be held in mind when defects are being pointed out. The upsurge of religious interest in America, evidenced by increases in church membership, attendance, giving, building, and popular status, is doubtless less than a Pentecost, but it is more than a promotional boom. At a minimum it gives the gospel a hearing, and so many persons would not be joining churches and working actively in them unless they believed it to be worth while.

Yet who can say that all those busily engaged in church work, whether clergy or laity, have a clear understanding of that to which they are devoting time and energy? As a result of lack of clear objectives motives fluctuate between a single-minded devotion to the glory of God and His service and a self-centered—though usually unconsciously self-centered—desire to enhance one's own prestige and status by activity in a highly respected social institution. Much of the relative ineffectiveness of today's churches in spite of the money and effort being poured into them can be traced to this dimness of understanding and hence diffusion of motivation.

A similar ambiguity exists in regard to the ecumenical movement. This is now firmly established and is making significant contributions through the World Council of Churches and other world-wide agencies, the National Council of the Churches of Christ in America, and many local councils. Yet it is a familiar and disturbing fact that ecumenical co-operation flourishes much better among the higher echelons of church leadership than at the local level. It cannot really function at its fullest or be most truly ecumenical until it gets into the blood of both clergy and laity at the local level. This it has done but incidentally.

There are various reasons for this situation. A practical reason is that anything *inter-* seems *extra,* and in the pressures of a busy society whatever energy is available gets funneled into the activities of one's own local congregation. This is enhanced by the fact that promotional zeal, whipped up through denominational leaders and boards, is denominationally oriented.

Yet a deeper reason for a lackadaisical or nonexistent ecumenicity in local churches stems from failure to understand the nature of the Church as the called and committed fellowship of Christ's followers, a fellowship spanning all national, racial, and cultural, as well as denominational lines, comprised of many households of faith yet with "one Lord, one faith, one baptism." A sense of togetherness among like-minded and congenial people does not of itself breed a sense of the reality of the world Christian community.

This situation is epitomized, on the one hand, in an easygoing tolerance which makes the oversimplified assertion, "It really does not matter what church you belong to. Instead of so many denominations we all ought to get together and have one big church." With this failure to recognize differences as well as agreements among churches there is seldom a deep devotion either to one's own denomination or to ecumenical effort. Yet traditional loyalties cut in from the opposite direction but with a similar result in the rejoinder, "Let those unite who want to—I love my church and I'll stick by it!"

These obstacles are a constant drag not only on organic mergers of churches locally and denominationally, but on the co-operative activities sponsored by the National Council and by local councils of churches. It would be folly to claim that a better understanding of the nature of the Church and of the place of the laity within it would overcome all of these obstacles, but it should somewhat clear the way for further ecumenical education and action to take place.

It is apparent that both local congregations and the ecumenical movement could profit from a more widespread inquiry as to what the Church is and what it exists for. But why make a special study of the status and function of the laity?

Here again we encounter a paradoxical situation, both at the local level and in the ecumenical movement. To comment first on the latter, it is the World Council of Churches that has taken the lead in arousing interest in this field, with one of the six main sections at the Evanston Assembly in 1954 devoted to "The Laity—The Christian in His Vocation" and with a department on the laity since that time. Yet the central point of discussion in the World Council's theological inquiries as to the nature of the Church has been the validity of a minister's—or priest's—ordination and hence his authority to administer the sacraments, especially the Lord's Supper. It is here that our deepest divisions lie, and such inquiries are very relevant to the possibility of taking communion together and hence symbolically manifesting our oneness in Christ. In this preoccupation with the ministry and the sacraments, however, attention to the laity has come almost as an afterthought.

To look more directly at the local church, nobody questions the fact that the laity is important in the sense that numerically laymen make up the greater part of its membership. They constitute over 99 per cent of it. Not only do they pay the minister's salary, but there is a general expectancy that some of them will render other services such as ushering, serving as officers in the many organizations, teaching in the church school, singing in the choir, working in the woman's society or the men's club.

These are useful services. But do laymen think of themselves as being the Church within the world in daily life? Do they regard themselves as being called by God to a ministry as important as that of the ordained clergy? Does "the priesthood of all believers" have meaning for them? In the early days of the Church all Christians were laity, differing in gifts and hence in functions but equal in status before God. Paul makes this quite clear in I Cor. 12. Do the laymen of today think of themselves as being as truly commissioned by the Spirit to Christian witness and service as are the clergy? In short, do they think of themselves as a major constituent in the reality of the Church?

The evidence appears to be to the contrary. In a recent survey of what Methodists believe, conducted by a research group of faculty members of Boston University School of Theology, an investigation was made at this point. Questionnaires were sent to a representative sampling of twelve thousand members of this denomination, covering a wide range of matters of Christian faith and its application to life. One of the categories was designed to test how laymen think of themselves. The following options were presented, of which the respondent was asked to check the one most nearly stating his own view:

Laymen are

members of the people of God called to a total ministry of witness and service in the world.

those who are ministered to by the clergy who are the true church.

people in part-time Christian service.
non-ordained Christians whose function is to help the clergy do the work of the church.

Of the 5,020 replies received, 59.9 per cent—by far the largest number—checked the fourth option. This appears to indicate that these laymen think of themselves primarily as assistants to the clergy, who if not the true church are at least the major element in it. Was this response due to modesty? Or to a long tradition, by no means limited to Methodism, of a clergy-centered church?

The fact is that the priesthood of all believers, so central to the Reformation, has never been taken seriously by churchmen. For reasons that will be stated later, it was not taken with full seriousness even by the Reformation leaders. Yet without depreciating the special functions and services of the ordained clergy, it is a great concept which ought to be taken seriously. Today, with the greater part of the fateful decisions which affect human life and destiny on this planet in the hands of laymen, it is more than ever imperative that its meaning be recovered.

Important beginnings have been made in this direction. One of these is in the relation of the layman's Christian faith to his daily work; that is, the viewing of economic and family life as the sphere of divine calling, which is the original meaning of vocation. Significant books in this field have been written by Elton Trueblood, Alexander Miller, Robert L. Calhoun, and others. In connection with vocational guidance under church auspices the idea has made considerable headway in America. In Europe much has been done through the laymen's institutes and evangelical academies to focus attention on the relations between Christian faith and the responsibilities of economic and political life.

A second important movement is in the direction of theology for laymen. Although, as is true in any advanced field of study, theological writing continues for the most part to be addressed to the writer's peers rather than to the common man, a considerable number of books have appeared in recent years which interpret the basic truths of the Christian faith in layman's language. Beginnings have also been made in setting up schools of religion which offer systematic courses in the Bible, Christian theology, church history, and Christian ethics for laymen. The layman who desires to plow in this field no longer lacks the tools.

These movements are bound to grow, and they merit all possible encouragement. A further description of them will be found in Chapters VII and VIII.

However, a theology *for* the laity is not the same thing as a theology *of* the laity, which calls for systematic study of the place of the laity within the nature of the Church. In this field by far the most influential book that has appeared, and in many respects a pioneer treatment, is Dr. Hendrik Kraemer's *A Theology of the Laity*.[1] This volume, which incorporates its author's Hulsean Lectures at Cambridge University in 1958, is a very suggestive one, and while I shall proceed along a quite different pattern, I gladly acknowledge my indebtedness to it. There is room for a further look at this important theme, and in particular for one that deals with it more specifically from the standpoint of the American churches in encounter with an opulent and complacent secularism.

I trust this brief introduction has made it apparent that an examination of the nature of the Church and of the status and function of the laity are not two separate issues. Though the first is the broader, the second is an important aspect of the first and dependent on it. To omit or subordinate consideration of the laity, as has traditionally been done in theoretical discussions of the nature and authority of the Church, is to truncate and distort our understanding. To consider "lay activities"

[1] Philadelphia: The Westminster Press, 1958.

without reference to a wider and deeper base is to reduce the layman's status to busy work in the churches and often to encourage the expenditure of precious time and energy in less than essential activities.

The reader must not expect to find the laity mentioned on every page. If this were a handbook on lay activities or a discussion of Christian vocations for laymen this could be done. This book has neither of these purposes, though it is tangent to both. What it aims primarily to do is to help laymen to have a better understanding of the Church and through this knowledge to have a better grasp of their own place in it. Accordingly, much will be said that speaks of the Church as a whole. Yet always in the author's mind, and let us hope in the reader's, the layman is there.

The first half of the book deals mainly with the nature of the Church—what it is, how its principal divisions came to be as they are, what its God-given functions are. The second and third chapters give a rapid historical survey of changes that have taken place from New Testament times to the emergence of the major Protestant denominations. In this historical setting the "priesthood of all believers" takes on meaning. Chapter IV, on the functions of the Church, deals both with the joint responsibilities of clergy and laity and with such differentiations of function as appear within an equality of status.

The remainder of the book is more directly related to the current scene. Chapters V and VI indicate reciprocally both the impingement of secular standards and practices upon the churches and some of the channels by which the Church can be a constructive force in the remaking of society. Chapters VII and VIII describe some projects and signs of hope, both in Europe and America, which point in the direction of a more effective participation by laymen as they endeavor to be the Church within the world. The brief concluding chapter suggests some basic considerations in the need for a unity that is not uniformity within and among the churches and in the relations of the churches to the society around them.

The book is addressed both to clergy and to laity—to the clergy for any light it may throw on their own commitment to Christ in His Church and the responsibilities of leadership, to lay men and women with the hope that it may serve in some measure to give new dignity to their calling and open up some new vistas of service. With no differentiation of status it was affirmed in the great days of the New Testament church, "But you are a chosen race, a royal priesthood, a holy nation, God's own people, that you may declare the wonderful deeds of him who called you out of darkness into his marvelous light" (I Pet. 2:9). To feel this glow and to witness to these wonderful deeds is a major need of our time, and the duty and privilege of us all.

Chapter I

WHAT IS THE CHURCH?

THIS CHAPTER WILL ATTEMPT TO SUGGEST AN ANSWER TO A question which on the surface looks disgustingly simple, yet under the surface comes near to being the most disputed point in Christian theology. It is too much to hope that all Christians will agree to what will be said in reply to the query, "What is the Church?" Yet we shall try in this chapter to keep to matters about which there is very large agreement, leaving the grounds of our divisions and differences to be dealt with later.

We shall be discussing ecclesiology, the doctrine of the nature of the Church. Like ecumenicity this is a term to get used to and is coming into more common usage as interest in the subject grows. It is a convenient short-cut, and we shall use it as the need arises.

Perhaps the reader will go to the dictionary. What he finds there may illustrate the lack of understanding to which even dictionary makers are sometimes subject! In one of my dictionaries I find two simple definitions: 1. The study of church institutions; 2. The science of building or decorating churches. In a fairly recent edition of Webster's dictionary the definition of ecclesiology is still further afield from its theological meaning: "The science of antiquities as applied to churches and other ecclesiastical foundations; the science and theory of church building and decoration."

This book will have very little to say about how churches should be built and decorated, though in a moment we shall note how the symbolism and general structure of a church speak to us of the purposes for which the Church exists. It may be observed in passing that one of the symptoms of sickness in the American church scene is that we are so much concerned with building and decorating and too little concerned with the worship and service that go on in the churches thus lavishly built and decorated. Neither architecture nor antiquities is our main interest in this book, however. Ecclesiology as we shall be considering it is an aspect of theology.

Yet to make our inquiry as practical as possible, suppose we ask a layman what he means when he says "my church," and note his replies. He may refer us to the building in which he worships on Sunday morning, to the congregation who worships there with various through-the-week activities for those who will participate in them, or to his denomination. Possibly, though not so probably, he may mean something larger than any of these—a world fellowship of Christians of which he feels himself a part.

He is right in all of these answers, though from different angles and perspectives. So let us look at each of them in turn.

1. THE CHURCH BUILDING

Ecclesiology as "the science of building or decorating churches" is not wholly unrelated to ecclesiology in its theological meaning. With some ultramodern exceptions a church ordinarily looks like a church. One can usually tell it from a house, a store, or a theater. It *ought* to look like a church if possible, though vital corporate worship has at times been maintained in all these structures or in none.

If our layman who is being interrogated looks around at the familiar aspects of his church building and asks himself why they are this way and not some other, the answers will point to some basic elements in ecclesiology.

On the outside there is usually a spire, pointing symbolically toward the Lord of heaven and earth to whom our upward-lifted prayer and praise ascend. The first note, then, about the Church is its God-centeredness; when it surrenders this primacy to become a man-centered institution, it loses its essential nature.

Sometimes on the outside of the building, and almost always inside the sanctuary, upon or above the altar, is the cross, the most sacred symbol of our Christian faith. Signifying the meeting point of suffering with love in the death of Christ for our salvation, calling Christ's followers to walk in the way of the cross in humble, willing obedience, it is central to the Church's meaning and mission.

Since the time of the Reformation the faithful preaching of the Word and the right administration of the sacraments have been regarded as essential marks of the true Church. In some churches the pulpit with an open Bible upon it stands at the center of a raised platform to emphasize the centrality of preaching. In others the altar with the cross is at the center of worship, with the pulpit and lectern on either side of the chancel. This is more than an architectural fancy; it symbolizes what is believed to be most basic.

At the altar or Communion table the most sacred of all Christian rites is celebrated to commemorate, or according to some forms of ecclesiology to reenact, the sacrifice of Christ for our redemption. Nearby is the baptismal font, symbol of cleansing from sin and entrance into the Christian fellowship, whether by the parents' dedication of their children or by the adult's vows of Christian discipleship.

Other elements often taken for granted say something about the nature of the Church. Because the people assemble to worship God and to hear the Word, the pews face the altar and pulpit. In the pews are hymnals, prayerbooks, and psalters, for it is not the preacher only, but also the congregation that has come to worship God with praise and prayer. In the more liturgical churches there will also be kneeling benches.

By long tradition there is a place in the sanctuary for the organ and choir. The choir is not there to give a concert, but to lead the people in worship through song and in the anthems to sing the praises of God in the holiness of beauty. Their responsibility as lay men and women is equal with the ministers' in making the service redound to the glory of God, and their calling was never better expressed than in the words of the psalmist:

> Sing to the Lord, bless his name;
> tell of his salvation from day to day.
>
> . . . .
>
> Honor and majesty are before him;
> strength and beauty are in his sanctuary. (Ps. 96:2, 6.)

Obviously what is rendered ought to be "comely praise"; yet it is not the aesthetic quality of the music, but the spirit of worship that is basic to the nature of the Church.

Less conspicuously placed but very important in Christian services are the offering plates. Inherent in the nature of the Church, but often too narrowly conceived, is the call to stewardship of all that we have received and hold in trust from God. The laymen who take the offering, as those who sing in the choir, have a high responsibility for making this part of the service of worship a meaningful act of dedication as the people offer themselves, as well as a portion of their material gifts received from God, to His honor, glory, and service.

Quite probably, our layman who is noting what the structure of the sanctuary can teach him of ecclesiology will discover other symbols in stained-glass windows and perhaps also in paintings, carvings, candles, and embroidered cloths bearing conventional letters or designs, each with great historic meaning. In a Quaker meetinghouse the setting will be plain and unadorned, with no Communion table or baptismal font. In a Baptist or Disciples church he will discover a baptistery which can be filled with water for baptism by immersion. In a Roman Catholic church he will see statuary suggesting the veneration of the saints, graphic representations of the stations of the Cross, confessional booths and many votive candles. This is not by accident or simply for decoration; it all has a meaning.[1]

It is not our purpose to trace all of these meanings here, though some of them we shall come to later as we note what makes churches differ from one another. Enough has been said to indicate that if one goes into a church and looks around with his eyes open, he will see enough to suggest a good deal about the nature and the distinctive purpose of the Church.

To summarize thus far, the Church exists for the worship and service of God. To this worship and service we are called by Christ, with the cross the focal point of His self-giving for our salvation. The Church, then, is the fellowship of Christ's followers. Christians assemble in the house of God, not for their own enjoyment or self-gratification, but to honor and praise God and thereby be impelled to serve Him more worthily within the world at the call of Christ. The Church is founded on the Word of God in the Bible, but beyond any written record is the Word in Christ Himself as God's supreme revelation and self-disclosure.

If, as Christians around the world declare in familiar words,

> The Church's one foundation
> Is Jesus Christ her Lord,

[1] See Thomas A. Stafford, *Christian Symbolism in the Evangelical Churches* (Nashville: Abingdon Press, 1942) for an excellent interpretation of historic Christian symbols.

then the Church has a distinctive message and mission, a source and a goal that make it different from any other social institution. If the cross is genuinely at its center and not merely a bit of conventional architectural adornment, then it must bear the burden of the world upon its heart.

And this the laity must do, for they are as truly a part of the Church's ministry—its service to the world in the name of Christ—as are its ordained servants.

2. THE CONGREGATION

Every layman knows that "my church" means more than the building in which he worships, more or less regularly, on Sunday morning; it means himself and the other people who assemble there. In fact, it means many more than can be found in church on any ordinary Sunday morning. But what, if anything, distinguishes those whose names are on the church membership lists, or if one wishes to narrow the question, who attend church with a fair degree of frequency, from the non-church segment of the population?

We have not attempted up to this point to define the term layman. We cannot fruitfully go further, however, without attempting to sharpen up its meaning.

In the ordinary meaning of the term, to which we must adhere for the sake of a common understanding, a layman is an unordained member of a church. Unless there is some special reason to draw a distinction between the sexes, we shall assume in this book that "layman" includes lay women as well as men.

In a broader use of the term outside religious circles a layman is an uninformed, uninitiated person having no special competence in the field under discussion. Thus, most clergymen are laymen in the fields of medicine, electronics, aeronautics, and a vast range of scientific knowledge. This would have no special bearing on this study save for an important fact;

namely, that in many areas, especially of economic life, the laymen in the churches often have more technical knowledge than the clergy. This does not mean that the layman sees more clearly than his minister the moral issues involved in a particular situation; it does mean that, being in closer touch with the concrete realities of the situation, the layman has the greater opportunity and responsibility for setting right whatever may be wrong.

Yet neither of these definitions represents the original Christian meaning of the term. In the New Testament the Greek word *laos* means "the people of God." The derivation of the word "lay" is from the Greek *laïkos* (Latin *laïcus*), signifying that a layman belongs to the chosen people of God. In the beginning there were no ordained clergy; all Christians were laymen. The derivation of the word clergy from *kleros,* meaning lot or inheritance, is more obscure, but it is certain that it did not mean originally what it now means. Says Dr. Hendrik Kraemer:

> In the New Testament the word "klèros" when it is used in regard to the new community in Christ is always meant as the body of men and women who share in God's gift of redemption and glory, which is their "inheritance" (klèros), because they are incorporated in the Son. There is no shimmer of an idea of a definite body, called Clergy.[2]

So, in the early days of the Christian Church, all that we now call laymen and clergy were of one status, equally important in the eyes of God, all together making up one fellowship. Within this fellowship there were varying gifts and hence diverse functions, such as apostles, prophets, evangelists, pastors, and teachers. (See Eph. 4:11.) Almost invariably we read into these terms a higher clerical status than that of the rank-and-file Christian of New Testament times, so conditioned are

[2] *Op. cit.*, p. 52.

we by long years of stratification. Yet in the beginning all were *laikoi;* the most common term for the members of the Christian brotherhood was "saint"; and the "saints in Caesar's household" were as much a part of the Christian ministry of witness and service as were those charged with the particular reponsibility of being deacons, presbyters, or in the latest New Testament writings, bishops.

To revert to the questionnaire on what Methodists believe, it will be recalled that one of the optional statements as to what constitutes a layman reads: "Layman are members of the people of God called to a total ministry of witness and service in the world." This is what in the New Testament sense a layman is. It is what in the fullest sense today a layman ought to be. It is not surprising that the lay members of a church do not usually think of themselves in this light, but it is very important that more and more should discover this meaning and make it applicable to themselves.

Is there not presumption, however, in referring to the Christian *laos,* the Christian fellowship, in short the congregation, as "the people of God"? It depends on where we put the emphasis. Every congregation, including of course that part of it which we now call the clergy, is composed of sinners, often tragically in rebellion against the will of God. With Martin Luther we must say of even the most saintly member of the Christian fellowship *simul justus et peccator* (at the same time justified and sinner). Yet we may still believe that God in Christ calls us to be "saints [that is, dedicated Christians] together with all those who in every place call on the name of our Lord Jesus Christ, both their Lord and ours" (I Cor. 1:2).

We who comprise a Christian congregation are "the people of God." To say that *we* are God's people and thus to look with self-righteous pride and a sense of superiority on others is to betray our calling and falsify our witness. But to say that we are *God's* people is to exalt Him and gratefully to acknowledge His supreme gift to us in Jesus Christ as Lord and Saviour. If we take this conviction seriously, then all of life is different, the Church has a new vitality, and the world is served.

To be a member of a church, if this relation is more than perfunctory, involves being a member of a worshiping congregation on Sunday morning. But it involves more than this. Hence, a look at the layman's other responsibilities is in order.

To a greater degree than in New Testament times—one may add, to a greater degree in America now than in any other part of the world—lay members of a congregation participate in the various organizations and activities of the church. From one point of view this is very good; from another, in it lurks a subtle peril. We should not want the layman to do less. In most cases he ought to be doing more, with the activities of the church engaging more members and spread on a broader base. Much of the vitality of the American churches, where they are vital, roots in this capacity to enlist the participation of laymen. Yet even so, there are dangers.

In our society as a whole, this is doubtless the most highly organized and activistic era in the world's history. In spite of our having more leisure than in many lands, this activism is characteristic of America. For this there are complex reasons. Central to them are the competitive aspects of a highly developed technological society, with almost everybody hurrying busily to get something done and if possible to get it done sooner and better than somebody else.

It is natural that this mood should have affected our churches, for the same persons are in the churches who are busy in many spheres of activity outside them. Much of this impulse to action is constructive, for it has prompted both clergy and laity to good works in building churches; raising money for these, for missions, and for the relief of suffering; promoting Christian education in the church schools; providing recreation and fellowship; and doing many other things that ought to be done. No activity in the Church with such objectives of Christian service ought to be curtailed.

Yet at some points this penchant for organization and activity requires safeguards. For one thing, there is always a danger of injecting into church work an attitude of "keeping up with the Joneses," measuring what is done by social expectancy and secular standards instead of seeking first the kingdom of God. When this occurs we are apt to forget that we are to serve and worship God and not the Church as an end in itself, to glorify Him and serve our fellow men, not seeking credit or recognition or being worried over matters of prestige.

A second danger lurks in the phrase "to put on a program." Church activities will, indeed, succeed better if they are carefully planned and placed within a comprehensive program. The alternative to programming is not a loose procedure of "hit or miss," for the result is usually to miss. Yet to a very disturbing degree, the program of the many lay groups within our churches do miss the objectives of the Kingdom by being built around small objectives—often those of secular society which make a church gathering not very different from what these same laymen would be exposed to in an "arm-chair travelogue," a P.T.A. meeting, a Rotary or Kiwanis Club. On such occasions the watchword, "Let the Church be the Church," is much in order.

A deeper and more subtle danger, which will not be corrected until we have broadened our sense of Christian vocation, is the very common tendency of the layman to think that his Christian service is limited to what he does in and for the Church. Valuable and necessary as these activities may be, it is by what he does in the world that his fullest witness and service are rendered. If those who know him cannot see that his Christian faith makes a difference in office, factory, laboratory, or home, they are not likely to be greatly impressed by what he does at church. His essential calling, whether or not it is so designated, is to present and to represent the Christian gospel by being unmistakably of the people of God within the world.

3. THE DENOMINATION

We are still on the question, "What is my church?" And we must move out to a wider circle than that of the local congregation or community. This is the "denomination" as we call it in America, the "communion" as it is called in many parts of the world, which represents a particular family within the larger household of faith.

In almost all the denominations there is a differentiation of function, which often amounts to a stratification of status, between ordained clergy and laity. How this came about will be looked at in the next two chapters. Yet it is the business of clergy and laity together in our time to try to understand the issues, heal the divisions, and enhance the values of the denominational structure of our churches.

Nowhere else in the world are there so many denominations as in America. The number varies from year to year, as mergers take place or new denominations are formed. There are over 250 of them, though in many instances these are families within families of churches, as in the 21 different brands of Methodists and the 27 of Baptists reported in the *Year Book of the American Churches*. Many of them are small and have names unfamiliar to members of the more conventional churches—for example, Duck River Baptists or Two-Seed-in-the-Spirit Predestinarian Baptists. All real Christians belong to the Church of God; yet this name has been pre-empted by a particular denomination and, with variations, by a considerable number of denominations. Even the attempt to submerge or eliminate denominations by having community churches ends up with what is virtually a new denomination, the Community Church movement. This follows the course taken a century and a half ago by the Disciples of Christ, which began as a "brotherhood" to replace denominations by a New Testament type of Christian fellowship and then proceeded to become one more denomination.

We probably have too many denominations in America, with many of them small sects or "splinter" groups; however, the situation is not so bad as it sounds. About 70 per cent of American Protestants are members of churches affiliated with the National Council of the Churches of Christ in America, and these churches working co-operatively from many angles exert far more influence than all of the small sects taken together. The only large and widely influential Protestant churches not members of the National Council are the Southern Baptist and the Missouri Synod Lutheran.

There are reasons why we have so many denominations, possibly not good enough reasons to justify the situation, but at least reasons to explain it. For one thing, despite the fact that the Roman Catholic Church is the largest single religious group in America, this country has always been predominantly Protestant, and the Protestant principle of religious liberty encourages freedom of opinion and, hence, proliferation of religious groups. This has been accented by the deeply imbedded democratic principle of the separation of Church and State and with it freedom of worship for all. Furthermore, America has long been known as "the melting-pot," the country receiving by immigration people from more national, racial, and religious groups than anywhere else in the world. Since church and culture are so closely intertwined, the transplanting of Old World, Near and Middle East, and in some cases Far East, church groups to these shores has increased the number of denominations.

One of the major concerns of the ecumenical movement is this splitting of the Church of Christ into so many divisions, not alone in this country but around the world. This is why

198 churches have now banded together to constitute the World Council of Churches, and 33 to form the National Council, with more being added from time to time. It should be understood that neither of these Councils is a super-church or aims to be one. It is not the purpose of either of these organizations to try to negotiate the mergers of churches—to become a "marriage mart" as it has been put. Yet in both of these Councils there is a Faith and Order Commission that studies the grounds of unity and is much concerned with the theological and other factors that keep the churches divided.

Both the World and the National Councils aim basically at promoting mutual understanding, Christian fellowship, and co-operative effort among the churches. Among their leaders, opinions vary widely as to the desirability of encouraging particular mergers among the denominations, though there is general agreement that this must not be done prematurely or without careful understanding of the grounds of existing differences. Yet there is also general agreement that the Body of Christ has been split apart, and this is not as it should be. One hears much of "the sin of our divisions." This requires us to ask whether having different denominations is really sinful, and perhaps to add a query as to whether the American churches are more sinful than others because we have so many more of them.

There certainly ought to be greater unity among the churches than now exists. As Christians we have "one Lord, one faith, one baptism," and granting the legitimacy of some differences of opinion as to interpretations of faith and modes of baptism, we still ought to find a greater unity in Christ. This unity ought to be both spiritual and visible—the more visible because of deeper spiritual bonds. Yet this is not to say that the existence of denominations is in its basic nature a sin against God or that it is wholly a barrier to the effective witness and service of the churches.

Whether such division is sinful depends on what causes it and what results from it. When groups split off from other groups of Christ's followers because of self-righteous pride or dogmatic intolerance or some such unholy barrier as racial prejudice, such division can well be said to be sinful. When these divisions are carried along with hard feelings and with aspersions cast toward other groups as being not Christian—or, at least, not as Christian as we are!—the effects can be very serious. At this point we do well to repent of the sinfulness of our divisions, provided repentance starts with ourselves and we bring forth fruits meet for repentance.

However, many of the major divisions of the Church have been the result of deep conscientious conviction, as the Protestant Reformation itself was. The Reformed and Anglican groups then accented certain notes that differed from the Lutheran. The Congregational and Baptist groups asserted the spirit of religious freedom against State control. The Methodist movement emerged to give a more vital evangelical witness than was found in eighteenth-century Anglicanism. We shall later have more to say about the grounds of these differences. In judging the merits and deficiences of our denominational diversity, it is important to bear in mind that whatever may be said of sporadic, fly-by-night movements that create new denominations, all of the major ones came into being because of some deep-seated historical and often theological reason. Instead of decrying their existence we do well to treasure what is good in this rich diversity within the household of faith.

Where the relations between churches are harmonious, this diversity within a Christ-centered unity is like a symphony in which all the instruments must play together, or like a rich mosaic or piece of tapestry in which each minor part contributes to the pattern of the whole. Nowhere have I seen the contributions of each group of the major families of faith more aptly stated than in a litany prepared some years ago by the Episcopal lay women's Society of Companions of the Holy Cross. It reads as follows, though for the sake of brevity I shall omit the response which is repeated after each affirmation of gratitude:

Let us give thanks for the gifts and graces of each great division of Christendom:

For the Roman Catholic Church; its glorious traditions; its disciplines in holiness; its worship, rich with the religious passion of the centuries; its noble company of martyrs, doctors and saints,

. . . .

For the Eastern Orthodox Church; its secret treasure of mystical experience; its marvelous liturgy; its regard for the collective life and its common will as a source of authority,

. . . .

For the great Protestant Communions:

For the Congregationalist jealousy for the rightful independence of the soul and of the group;

For the stress in the Baptist Churches upon personal regeneration and upon the conscious relation of the mature soul to its Lord;

For the power of the Methodists to awaken the conscience of Christians to our social evils; and for their emphasis upon the witness of personal experience, and upon the power of the disciplined life,

. . . .

For the Presbyterian reverence for the Sovereignty of God and their confidence in His faithfulness to His covenant; for their sense of the moral law, expressing itself in constitutional government;

For the witness to the perpetual Real Presence of the Inner Light in every human soul borne by the Religious Society of Friends, and for their faithful continuance of a free prophetic ministry,

. . . .

For the Lutheran Church; its devotion to the Grace of God and the Word of God, enshrined in the Ministry of the Word and Sacraments,

. . . .

For the Anglican Church; its reverent and temperate ways, through its Catholic heritage and its Protestant conscience; its yearning concern over the divisions of Christendom, and its longing to be used as a house of Reconciliation,

We thank Thee, O Lord, and bless Thy Holy Name.[3]

4. THE CHURCH UNIVERSAL

We must now look at the meaning of that which is broader than any denomination, even the largest of them—in short, not at the churches but at the Church.

Implicitly, the layman knows that he means something more inclusive than his local congregation or his own denomination when he speaks of the Church. How much more he means by it will depend somewhat on the nature of the assumptions in his own church—for example, the Roman Catholic Church thinks of itself as the only true church and some Protestant authoritarian groups foster this same opinion of themselves. Ordinarily, however, the breadth of meaning a Protestant puts into the term will depend on the degree to which his vision has been enlarged and his mind stretched by knowledge of the Church of Christ around the world. One of the greatest contributions of both the missionary and the ecumenical movements has been this enlargement of vision and with it a deeper sense of fellowship with the Christians of many lands.

Let us look at the Church in this broad sense by examining some of the terms used to describe it. To begin with one already

[3] "Thanksgiving for Our Unity in Christ," *Federal Council Bulletin,* XXIII, 2 (February, 1940). Used by permission of Mrs. D. Trumbull Huntington, Society of Companions of the Holy Cross.

used, the word "ecumenical," let it be clear that, strictly speaking, there is no "ecumenical church" though there is a very important "ecumenical movement." It comes from the Greek word *oikumene,* meaning an assemblage "from the inhabited world." In the early centuries of the Church there were some very important ecumenical councils bringing together churchmen from what was then the entire Christian world to decide some basic issues of theology. In the twentieth century ecumenicity has again come into the foreground of Christian thought to promote co-operative study and action among the major Protestant and Eastern Orthodox churches. Yet this movement is not itself the Church; it aims rather to be an instrument of the Church universal.

"The Church universal" is a very rich and meaningful term which conveys the thought that the Church of Christ is intended by God to be universal throughout the world, permeating the whole of life, unrestricted by any human barriers such as differences of nation, race, color, economic status, or culture. This does not mean that the Church as it now exists is universal. In a quip sometimes quoted in ecumenical circles a cynic is said to have remarked, "I believe in the Church universal and regret that it does not exist." Yet the Church universal, we may well believe, is the true nature of the Christian fellowship, God's design for it. It is epitomized in the great commission, "Go therefore and make disciples of all nations." It is a goal not yet fully attained, but it is increasingly being brought to fulfilment as the gospel is taken to new fields throughout the world and the ecumenical movement unites in closer fellowship the existing churches.

Another familiar phrase expressing the same idea from a different angle is the affirmation of the Apostles' Creed, "I believe in . . . the holy catholic Church, the communion of saints." These two declarations belong together and in reality constitute one affirmation, the second explanatory of the first.

The communion of saints does not, as we often assume, mean solely the assemblage in heaven of "all the saints who from their labors rest." It includes these, but it means the fellowship of the faithful, both those who have passed from the earthly scene and those now living. Together they constitute the holy catholic Church, the Church of Christ for time and eternity.

But is the Church holy? And is it catholic? To begin with the second of these terms, for we have already touched on it in looking at the Church universal, the Church is catholic in the basic meaning of this word as inclusive and universal. It is important that we spell it with a small "c," for to use a capital letter is to make it refer to the churches that call themselves Catholic from their belief that they get their authority from Christ through the apostolic succession—that is, the Roman Catholic, Eastern Orthodox, Anglican, and Old Catholic churches.[4] Actually, to use the term "catholic" in this exclusive sense is from the standpoint of other Christians a less catholic position than is warranted by the ideal of the Church universal.

To say that the Church is holy, like saying that it is catholic, is not to declare that it is now perfectly holy or just as it ought to be in God's sight. Every existing church, being composed of Christians who are sinners, has elements of sin within it. To call it holy means that it is meant by God to be holy, led and empowered by the Holy Spirit, and commissioned with a sacred duty to be the carrier of Christ's gospel to all men and to all of life. In short, it is not simply one more social institution among the many we have in our society; it has a particular message and a particular mission. We may well believe also that it has a God-given destiny and that in spite of the assaults of evil

[4] The Old Catholic Churches are a relatively small group of European churches, mainly in Holland with some in Germany and Switzerland, that began in 1700 to dispute the power of the Pope. In 1870 they rejected the dogma of papal infallibility and established a separate denomination under the Convention of Utrecht in 1889. In theology, ritual, and canon law they are much like the Roman Catholic Church.

men and evil forces upon it "the power of death shall not prevail against it" (Matt. 16:18).

The four historic "notes" of the Church, as these are stated in the Nicene Creed and affirmed repeatedly by both Catholics and Protestants, are that it is "one, holy, catholic and apostolic." As must already be evident, these terms are understood differently by Catholics and Protestants. A term used by both groups as something of a short-cut for the one holy universal Church is the *una sancta*. It is an ambiguous term, the full definition of which would involve the many shades of difference in understanding as to the nature of the Church.

In what sense is the Church *apostolic?* This is important, for it is basic to the authority of the existing, visible Church. Those churches holding to the apostolic succession through the laying on of hands as the ground of the historical continuity of the bishops, and hence of the validity of the ministry and sacraments through ordination by a bishop in this succession, trace it to Christ's commissioning of the apostles. The Roman Catholic Church finds its authority in our Lord's words to Peter as stated in Matt. 16:18-19; others vary as to the degree to which these words are taken literally but still believe in a divine authority for this form of visible continuity of the Church's existence. Most Protestants, on the other hand, regard the Church as apostolic in the sense that we share in the faith of the first apostles and like them are commissioned to carry Christ's message to the world, but without holding to any external form of continuity as mandatory for all churches. This kind of apostolicity is basic to the theme of this book, for in the apostolic continuity of witness and service, laymen, though unordained, are still called as are the clergy to be Christ's apostles in the world of today. This is the essential meaning of the priesthood of all believers.[5]

[5] Further explanation of this term will be given when its historical origins are presented in Chapter III.

Another great term for the Church, found both in the Bible and in much current discussion, is "the Body of Christ." Paul uses it in Rom. 12:4-5 and again in I Cor. 12:12-30 to indicate that just as the body must have all of its parts working together, each with its own function, so the Church as Christ's body has members of many differing gifts but each with an essential place. In Eph. 4:12 there is a moving exhortation to use these gifts "for the equipment of the saints, for the work of ministry, for building up the body of Christ."

This term is not the only one in the Bible to designate the nature of the Church. Paul S. Minear in a careful search of the New Testament has found more than eighty of them.[6] It is a very apt term, however, and it would be hard to find a better analogy. It emphasizes not only the interrelatedness of all members of the Church—and by implication, the relatedness of denominations to each other—but also another fact of supreme importance: *The Church is that body of which Christ is the Head.* Whenever a church loses sight of the headship of Christ, it becomes a social institution doing some good works which might equally well be done by some other group and is on its way to becoming simply a secular club of respectable and congenial people.

The Church is also sometimes referred to as the *New Israel.* This means that just as we have continuity between the Old and New Testaments (meaning the old and new covenants), so there is continuity between God's plan and purpose in His covenant with Israel as the chosen people and His plan and purpose for the Church in the redemption of the world as it becomes the carrier of Christ's gospel. In taking the message and work of Christ to the world, the Church is God's chosen

[6] See his brochure prepared for the World Council of Churches' Theological Commission on Christ and the Church, and expanded in his book *Images of the Church in the New Testament* (Philadelphia: The Westminster Press, 1960).

instrument. This puts great meaning and depth into the familiar passage in I Peter:

> But you are a chosen race, a royal priesthood, a holy nation, God's own people, that you may declare the wonderful deeds of him who called you out of darkness into his marvelous light. Once you were no people but now you are God's people; once you had not received mercy but now you have received mercy. (I Pet. 2:9-10.)

If this is our high calling, we had better not be self-centered or lackadaisical about it!

Two other Greek terms suggest something very important about the nature of the Church. These are *koinonia* and *ekklesia. Koinonia* means "community," *ekklesia* "an assembly of those called out." Put these words together, and it means that the Church is a community or fellowship of Christ's followers, redeemed through His saving love and called to witness and service in His name.

We often use the term community to mean simply the geographical location in which we live. In a deeper sense, community means fellowship, mutual concern, a sense of brotherhood and of belonging to one another. This is what the Church of Christ in its true nature is, and as our vision and sympathy and sense of fellowship broadens we understand better the meaning of another term for the Church universal, the "world Christian community." This meaning may well come home to us with special vividness as we participate in the observance of World-wide Communion Sunday the first Sunday in October or the World Day of Prayer the first Friday in Lent. Yet not on special days only, but every day, we should be prompted to thank God for this world-wide fellowship in Christ of which each local congregation and each individual Christian is a part.

The term *ekklesia* has become curiously twisted, for the word "ecclesiastical" has come to mean, not the vital fellowship of those called out to membership in Christ's Church, but the formal elements in the practices and polity of the Church. The latter we must have, but it is a serious matter when the organizational structure of the Church takes precedence over its basic functions. When this happens it is a short step to the following of secular motives, pulls, and pressures; in short, to yielding within the activities of a church to the interests and standards of the world around us instead of listening to the call and doing the work of Christ. At this point—and this means many points in the life and thought of the churches of today—we need to hear again the words of Paul, "Do not be conformed to this world but be transformed by the renewal of your mind, that you may prove what is the will of God, what is good and acceptable and perfect" (Rom. 12:2).

To sum up, the Church is first of all a fellowship—a distinctive fellowship of those redeemed by Christ and called by Him to worship God and to serve our fellow men. It is secondarily an institution, fulfilling its proper function only as God is glorified, men are served in love, and Christ is exalted as Head of His Church. To take these convictions seriously might involve some large-scale changes in present practices within our churches.

Chapter II

HOW OUR DIVISIONS CAME ABOUT—ROMAN AND EASTERN

In this chapter and the next we shall be trying to serve two purposes at once, combining them not only to avoid repetition, but also to point out their intimate connection. One of these purposes will be to trace rapidly in outline the most important steps by which we got our various denominations. If we understand how we came to be as we are in the present divided state of the Church, we shall know better how to judge these differences and what it is feasible to undertake as we seek to move toward a closer unity.

Yet there is another sense in which the Church is divided. This is the stratification which puts the clergy in one category and the laity in another, with the almost universal subordination of the laity as one thinks about the Church. This does not follow completely the pattern of the emergence of the denominations, but is related to it. We shall note as we proceed what these relations are.

To tell in detail the story of the emergence of the denominations, to say nothing of the place of the laity within them, would mean tracing the entire history of Christianity. This it is obviously impossible to do in a book as brief as this one. It is hoped that the reader who may not be familiar with the history of the Church will turn to one or more of the many good books available and make this important and fascinating story a vital part of his mental storehouse.[1]

[1] Though more recent books have been written, Williston Walker, *The History of the Christian Church* (New York: Charles Scribner's Sons, 1918, rev. ed. 1959)

1. THE CHURCH OF THE NEW TESTAMENT

In the church of New Testament times, often called the primitive church and the times, the Apostolic Age, there were no denominations as we now know them. Yet there were divisions. Paul made this evident when he said at the beginning of his letter to the church at Corinth:

> For it has been reported to me by Chloe's people that there is quarreling among you, my brethren. What I mean is that each one of you says, "I belong to Paul," or "I belong to Apollos," or "I belong to Cephas," or "I belong to Christ." Is Christ divided? Was Paul crucified for you? Or were you baptized in the name of Paul? (I Cor. 1:11-13.)

In addition to such personal tensions there was uneasiness over the question as to whether Gentile converts must submit to Jewish rites, and while this was officially settled in the negative in a conference of great historic importance recorded in Acts 15, it kept cropping up. Paul wrote the letter to the Galatians because he had learned that certain Judaizers were attempting to revive this issue and were disturbing the unity of the church. (See Gal. 1:6-9.) There are great affirmations of unity in the book of Ephesians in such statements as "one Lord, one faith, one baptism" (4:5), and "For he is our peace, who has made us both one, and has broken down the dividing wall of hostility" (2:14). Yet these affirmations themselves suggest a unity among the people so uncertain or disrupted that the followers of Christ needed to be called to their true unity in Christ. Had this unity been an established fact, it could have been taken for granted without the necessity to speak of it so often.

---

and Arthur W. Nagler, *The Church in History* (New York: The Abingdon Press, 1929) still seem to me the most usable general surveys of church history. Roland H. Bainton, *The Church of Our Fathers* (New York: Charles Scribner's Sons, 1941) was written originally for children and young people but has been widely used by adults and is an unusually simple and readable presentation.

John Knox in *The Early Church and the Coming Great Church* has shown conclusively from the New Testament and the writings of the early church fathers that there were differences then not only of personal opinion, but also of forms of worship, theology, and polity. There were bonds of unity as well, but no single-track or monolithic unity. He sums it up as follows:

> The situation was in flux: congregations were related more or less closely with other congregations, sharing in varying degrees in common traditions, beliefs, and practices, acknowledging the validity of some of the same norms and the authority of some of the same persons; but there was wide diversity in both cult and faith, and signs of tension and of actual division, both within and among congregations, are not lacking.[2]

The importance of this for today lies in the fact that when we claim authority for some fixed type of ecclesiology on the basis of going back to "the undivided church," we are trying to go back to what never existed. Even when more modestly we yearn for "the reunion of Christendom," what we are really seeking is union, not reunion. "There has never been a time when the church could be truly said to be united." [3]

As was indicated in the previous chapter, there are references in the New Testament to a variety of gifts and forms of service in the Church. There is the list in Eph. 4:11, "And his gifts were that some should be apostles, some prophets, some evangelists, some pastors and teachers, for the equipment of the saints, for the work of ministry, for building up the body of Christ." There is a longer list in I Cor. 12:28, "And God has appointed in the church first apostles, second prophets, third teachers, then workers of miracles, then healers, helpers, administrators, speakers in various kinds of tongues."

[2] Nashville: Abingdon Press, 1955, p. 13.
[3] *Ibid.*, p. 12.

It cannot be too strongly emphasized that at that time, all of these people were of the laity. To be of the *laos,* the people of God, and hence followers of Christ in witness and service, was all the honor or privilege that was felt to be needed. It has been persuasively pointed out that since the original Greek has no commas, the Ephesians passage in stating the reasons for these gifts ought to read, "for the equipment of the saints for the work of ministry." [4] Certainly it does not say "the ministry" in the *kleros* sense, and we ought not to read this meaning into it. Similarly in the Corinthians passage there is no reason to assume that the apostles, prophets, and possibly teachers were ordained clergy while the rest were not.

There are also references in the New Testament, however, to deacons, to elders or presbyters, and to bishops. These references have been made the basis for the claim of a threefold ministry as apostolic and therefore mandatory for all time. It is in order to take a look at this claim.

The word "deacon" means "helper" or "servant." It is clear enough how there came to be deacons, for Acts 6:1-6 tells the story. The Gentile, that is, the Greek Christians became disturbed because they thought their widows were not getting their proper share in the daily distribution of food. But who was to take care of the matter? The twelve apostles called a meeting of the congregation and said to them, "It is not right that we should give up preaching the word of God to serve tables. Therefore, brethren, pick out from among you seven men of good repute, full of the Spirit and of wisdom, whom we may appoint to this duty. But we will devote ourselves to prayer and to the ministry of the word" (Acts 6:2-4).

It is also stated that when the people had chosen these seven, of whom Stephen is the first named as well as presently the first martyr, the apostles prayed and laid their hands upon them.

[4] William Robinson, *Completing the Reformation* (Lexington, Ky.: College of the Bible, 1955), p. 21.

This is apparently the beginning of the practice in ordination of the laying on of hands, though it is very doubtful that in the initial act it was thought of as an ecclesiastical rite that would continue through the centuries. More likely, it was an act of friendly commendation and expression of confidence. Could the apostles have foreseen that nearly twenty centuries later, their act would be a source of division and even of sharp contention in the Church they would doubtless have been greatly astonished.

Since all of the seven deacons chosen on this occasion have Greek names, the incident reflects a cultural cleavage. The Greeks were to look after the menial tasks while the Jewish Christians did the preaching! But it did not work out that way. These Greek deacons saw their service (*diakonia*) as something more inclusive—as an obligation to witness to the gospel. So Stephen, "full of grace and power, did great wonders and signs among the people," and because of his evangelizing with such ardor he was attacked, was charged with blasphemy, and after preaching one of the greatest sermons ever delivered, was stoned to death. The effect of this witness on a young man, Saul of Tarsus, who guarded the garments of those who stoned him and "was consenting to his death," is one of the most dramatic and crucial in Christian history.

Was Stephen a layman or a minister, in the usual meaning of these terms? All we can say is that he was very much of "the people of God" and very much a "minister" in his witness and service in the name of Christ.

We are given no such detailed account of how elders, often designated as presbyters, came to exist in the early church. They were apparently regarded as leading members of the congregation, comparable in status to the Jewish elders who are referred to many times in both the Old and New Testaments. The nearest approach to an account of how there came to be Christian elders is in Acts 14:23, where we are told that Paul and

Barnabas after having preached the gospel and made many disciples in Derbe, Lystra, Iconium, and Antioch appointed elders to look after these young churches. "And when they had appointed elders for them in every church, with prayer and fasting, they committed them to the Lord in whom they believed." In these few words we have the spiritually meaningful but ecclesiastically slender basis of what was later in some churches to become the priesthood, in others the body of leading laymen.

The elders reappear again and again in the New Testament, but we get little information as to their special duties. It need not surprise us that the New Testament does not say whether to regard them as priests or laymen, for as in the case of deacons all were laymen and all were ministers in the sense of being servants of God. All we can say of them with certainty is that they were Christians who held positions of responsible leadership.

Still less can we trace the origin of bishops. A bishop means an "overseer." But were the bishops over the elders? Or were the bishops the same as the elders? Here opinions differ, but with the evidence in the New Testament strongly tilted in the latter direction. Paul addresses his letter to the Philippians to "all the saints in Christ Jesus who are at Philippi, with the bishops and deacons" (1:1). Why leave out the elders, if there was then a threefold ministry? By the time of the latest New Testament writings, the letters to Timothy and Titus,[5] the bishops had risen to a position of considerable prominence. But even here they are not clearly distinguished from elders. In I Tim. 3 the qualifications of bishops and of deacons are given, but with no

[5] It is impossible to date these pastoral epistles with accuracy, but they contain references to conditions in the church which indicate a later setting than the time of Paul. "If a date must be suggested, A.D. 130-150 would seem to be a reasonable conjecture." Fred D. Gealy, *The Interpreter's Bible* (Nashville: Abingdon Press, 1955), XI, 370.

mention of elders. In Titus 1:5-9 both elders and bishops are spoken of but the terms appear to be synonyms.

It seems most likely that the office of bishop emerged as an extension of the office of elder. As the number of churches increased, a respected or otherwise influential elder who was at first the "overseer" of one congregation might come to have oversight over other churches in the same region, and the diocese came into being. How this happened, however, the literature of the period does not tell us. To quote a quip which I hope will offend the dignity of no living bishop:

> It has been said in jest that at the end of the apostolic age the church was like a locomotive going into a dark tunnel and that it emerged in the post-apostolic period with a bishop on its cow-catcher. All we can say with certainty is that at some point one of the presbyters rose to the position of "president" or representative of his colleagues, and to distinguish his office from the rest of the presbyters he was given the title of bishop.[6]

Yet this is not how the Roman Catholic Church looks at the office of bishop, and in particular its chief bishop, the pope. So, what happened next?

2. THE ROMAN CATHOLIC CHURCH

It is often assumed that the Roman Catholic Church emerged immediately out of the apostolic period on the basis of Christ's commission to Peter in Matt. 16:18-19. This is not the case. There was a period of fluidity which Protestants can claim as their heritage as truly as can Catholics. Yet forces were in operation, mainly from the second to the fifth centuries, which crystallized the Roman Church into the basic structure it has retained to the present. To see how these changes took place the reader will do well to consult the chapters on "How

[6] Howard Clark Kee and Franklin W. Young, *Understanding the New Testament* (Englewood Cliffs, N. J.: Prentice-Hall, Inc., 1957), p. 363.

Christianity Became Catholic" and "How Catholicism Became Roman" in Jaroslav Pelikan's *The Riddle of Roman Catholicism,*[7] but any good church history will supply the details.

We shall summarize these developments from the standpoint of the emergence of the priesthood and its sharp differentiation from the rank-and-file Christians; for, before long, there was such a priesthood. Furthermore, there were forces moving toward the exalting of the office of bishop above both ordinary parish priests and lay people, and eventually to the exalting of the bishop of Rome, believed to be Peter's successor, as pope and head over all.

Among these forces the principal ones are to be found in the missionary outreach of the Church, the need of an institutional structure, the need to formulate official doctrine as a norm for judging heresy, the emergence of a sacramental system of salvation with the consequent need of the proper offices to mediate it to the people, and all of these intertwined with a scriptural backlog and with current political and social forces. It was an enormously complex movement! Yet a brief look at each of these factors must suffice.

The primitive church was catholic—that is, universal in its outreach—in the best sense. Paul's missionary journeys and his letters to the young churches indicate this, and the martyrdoms of Ignatius of Antioch, Polycarp of Smyrna, Justin Martyr, and countless other nameless Christians who died for their faith in the fires of persecution attest it. In the book of Acts we read that "those who were scattered went about preaching the word" (8:4), and in the second century Justin states that "there is not a single race of men, . . . among whom prayers and thanksgivings are not offered through the name of the crucified Jesus to the Father and Maker of all things." [8] Regardless of the fact that this was not literally true, for Justin's world was much smaller

[7] Nashville: Abingdon Press, 1959.
[8] *Dialogue with Trypho,* 117.

than ours, the Church of the first and second centuries shows an amazing expansion in the face of obstacles.

This expansion called for leadership, for each new congregation or regional area must have its overseer, its bishop. Though it is not likely that Peter was ever the pontifical bishop of Rome in the sense in which the Church has usually understood the term, it is quite possible that for a time he was its leader. It seems certain from the New Testament that in the beginning Jerusalem was the mother church, with James as its administrative head, and that Peter did not found the church at Rome, since there is no mention of him in Paul's letter to the Romans. Yet Peter was the most dynamic of all the twelve apostles, and if he went to Rome his energy and zeal would make him its natural leader. Tradition says that both he and Paul were martyred there, and there is no strong reason to doubt it.

Early in the second century "catholic" began to mean "Catholic." The earliest Christian writing outside the New Testament which has been preserved to us is a letter from Clement, reputed to have been the fourth bishop of Rome, to the church at Corinth about A.D. 96. In this he pleads for a loyal submission to the authority of the bishop as a means of curtailing dissension and heresy and asserts that the twelve apostles had appointed the bishops as their successors. This authority was forcefully accented by Ignatius, bishop of Antioch, who was martyred in 117, and was reinforced by Irenaeus about A.D. 180. It was then seldom questioned until the Protestant Reformation. Thus with slender historical foundations the doctrine of the apostolic succession, which continues to divide churches today, emerged.

To pass to another aspect of what was happening, the missionary-minded catholic church in becoming Catholic had to have an institutional structure. A spirit does not function without a body, even though it is the Body of Christ. In addition to what the New Testament tells us of deacons and presbyter-bishops, the *Didache,* a Christian manual of instruction dating from the early second century, speaks of "bishops and deacons, your honorable men, alongside of your prophets and teachers." The bishops, some of whom were very honorable and saintly men while others were political aspirants seeking their own power, were soon to be *over,* not *alongside of,* those Christians with other gifts and graces. When this happened the "monarchical episcopacy" emerged and has remained a basic part of the Roman Catholic Church and some other forms of Catholicism to the present.

Obviously, the bishops could not be everywhere and in direct touch with the people. For this purpose it was natural enough that they should ordain parish priests. Nobody could be ordained to the priesthood except by the laying on of hands of a bishop, whose authority was believed to come in direct succession from the apostles, whose authority came from Christ. Thus something of the prestige and exalted status of the bishop was thought to be transmitted to the priest, a quality of sanctity which no layman not thus ordained could possibly possess.

When this happened the laity, far from being as in New Testament times the people of God with no stratification though with varying functions, were now definitely in a class by themselves. The clergy were in another class. This might not have been so serious save for the fact that the laity were now definitely *under* the clergy, under them in power and authority, in ecclesiastical status, and supposedly in the Christian life and in the moral demands expected of them. From this subordination the laity has never really recovered, and this book is being written because of this fact.

The crystallizing of the doctrine of the apostolic succession, with the resultant stratification of the levels of piety and power within the Church, did not happen all at once. The classical formulation of this theory was given by Cyprian in the third century. Nevertheless, the process once started was virtually inevitable. The delicate balance along the way is epitomized in Irenaeus, who was one of the major architects of the Church's ecclesiastical system, yet nevertheless could write, "all the righteous possess the sacerdotal rank," and "all the disciples of the Lord are Levites and priests." [9]

A third factor in the development of Roman Catholicism away from the vital fluidity of the apostolic church was the outcropping of heresy and the need of an authoritative body of truth against which to quench it. There was nothing indecisive or slippery about Paul's interpretation of the gospel message; yet he could write to the Corinthians, "Now the Lord is the Spirit, and where the Spirit of the Lord is, there is freedom." (II Cor. 3:17) . No such appeal to the liberty of the Spirit could satisfy the now solidifying, hierarchical Church.

The theology of the ancient church, however abstract and even hairsplitting it may seem to be to the modern mind, came into being for a very practical purpose—or more accurately, a double purpose with two related centers. It was wrought out in the crucible of history to defend the integrity of the gospel faith against such heresies as Gnosticism and Marcionism.[10] Likewise, it was expounded to commend the Christian faith to intellectuals of the Greco-Roman world and to demonstrate that Christianity was not at variance with other great systems of thought, but was superior to any. Both motives formed an important spur to clear thinking and defense, but with differing results.

There could be no unity in the Church if every Christian interpreted the Scriptures, or even the creeds as they became

[9] Kraemer, *op. cit.,* p. 56.

[10] Gnosticism was an eclectic form of theosophical speculation emphasizing a special secret knowledge (*gnosis*) as essential to salvation. It held a Docetic view of Christ—that is, that his humanity was not real but only an appearance. Regarding creation its exponents taught that the world is too evil to have been created by the supreme God of purity and love and is the product of a lesser deity. Marcion was semi-Gnostic in his views, stressing sharply a dualism between the God of the Old Testament and that of the New.

fomulated, to suit himself. Who then was to speak the authoritative word? Obviously the head of the Church, the bishop. Here the apostolic succession as preserver of the institution joins hands with the apostolic succession as custodian of truth. Not all the bishops could agree, however, and there could not often be a great ecumenical Council like that at Nicaea. The way was rapidly being paved for the elevation of one bishop over all the other bishops, but before we note how the bishop of Rome became the pope, we must take a look at the sacramental system.

Though the Roman Church was later to have seven sacraments, it had at the beginning, as most Protestant churches do today, the two sacraments of baptism and the Lord's Supper. Not only were these regarded as sacred rites from having been instituted by our Lord, but they were a great uniting force in binding the Christian fellowship together. They ministered deeply to the inner lives of Christians, kept the Church connected with its historical foundation in the life and death of our Lord, and prevented the Church from becoming simply a mystery cult like those all around it in the Greco-Roman world. All of these services except the last the sacraments still render, and we may rejoice that the Church had them.

Who was to administer and celebrate these sacraments to give them their proper sanctity? Certainly not just anybody. Who but a priest ordained by a bishop, who stood in the succession of the apostles, who in turn baptized at the behest of Jesus and received the Last Supper from His own hand? Granted the premises, the conclusion was wholly logical. Once more the laity are made subordinate, worthy to receive the sacrament under certain conditions set by the Church, but never to administer it. With this development there emerged a sacramental system of salvation giving immense power to the clergy, for to excommunicate is to close the doors to heaven as well to sever the most precious earthly ties.

This tightening of the hold of the Church upon its laity through the sacraments was, like everything else, a growing process and intertwined with other developments. It was Cyprian, bishop of Carthage, who in the middle of the third century set forth the classic doctrine of the Church epitomized in the words, *"Extra ecclesiam nulla salus"* (outside the Church there is no salvation). He has been called "the father of sacerdotalism," for he taught that the Church could not exist without the priesthood and that the priesthood controlled the keys to heaven and hell. The priesthood had no authority apart from the episcopacy, however; hence no bishop, no Church. The further step—that all bishops must have one head, and this head the bishop of Rome—was not yet taken, but events were tending in this direction.

So, we must now ask how the Catholic Church became Roman. The two developments were in process together, though the second came to completion later than the first and by stages less clearly marked.

We noted earlier that while there is no certainty that Peter was ever bishop of Rome his leadership there is an open possibility, and it is certain that he was the foremost of all the twelve apostles. In every list of them—whether of the twelve or of the more intimate three—he is the first named, and it was he who preached the great sermon at Pentecost when the Church was born. It is natural enough that the Roman church should have assumed Peter to be the "rock" (Matt. 16:18) on which the Church was to be founded, though Protestants were later to consider the rock to be Peter's great declaration that Christ is the Son of the living God.

Yet for the emergence of the church at Rome to primacy over all others, we must look to political and social rather than to biblical foundations. At the beginning, the church at Jerusalem was the "headquarters" of the Church, with Antioch a close second. So it remained until after the close of the New Testament period.

Rome was the seat of government, the "eternal city" with a glamor and greatness that still cling to it today. As the seat of government it was the place where the fires of persecution blazed most brightly, and in Tertullian's oft-quoted phrase, the blood of the martyrs became the seed of the Church. Either in spite of or because of such persecution there developed in Rome a vigorous metropolitan church. When the Emperor Constantine espoused Christianity and the Church came under state patronage in 313, its inner fabric was tested but its outer status was secure. When in 330 Constantine tried to decentralize his empire by moving the capital to Constantinople, the church at Rome remained strong, less shaken by the move than was the Roman political structure. When in the fifth century the Roman Empire was about to fall apart under invaders from the north, the "city of God"—the Church of which Augustine had written—stood firm.[11]

In view of these circumstances, it was natural enough that the prestige of the Roman name should be linked with the biblical affirmation of Christ's commission to Peter and the tradition that Peter had been the first bishop of the Roman church. It was a short step to the assumption that the bishop of Rome was henceforth to be known as the Pope, the direct representative of Christ on earth and the spiritual and temporal head of the Church.

This gave to priesthood and laity alike a center of loyalty and a rallying point for their faith. But it was not all smooth sailing thereafter. There were contests and problems in store, both as to who should be acknowledged as the rightful pope and still more often, who was to be the more powerful, pope or emperor. Much of the history of the medieval period centers around this

[11] In fairness to Augustine it should be noted that he did not completely identify the visible Church with the city of God.

question of the supremacy of Church or State. It is still a live issue, and laymen even today must ask themselves whether two sovereignties—that of the nation and that of the Vatican—are compatible. These questions we must leave aside for the present and look at the next divisions that took place within the Church.

3. EARLY VARIATIONS

There were numerous groups that split off from the main stream of the Church in the early centuries of its formation which flourished for awhile and then died out. Most of these did not achieve the status of separate churches, but were the stirrings of dissenting groups over matters of doctrine or policy. Among these were the Ebionites, who wanted to exclude non-Jews and keep Christianity Jewish; the Marcionites, who were anti-Jewish at the point of giving little respect or credence to the Old Testament; the Montanists, who were a good deal like the Pentecostals of the present; the Manichaeans, who held to a weird mixture of Persian religion and Greek philosophy with a sprinkling of Christianity thrown in; the Donatists, who maintained that the validity of the sacraments depended not only on the right ordination of the priest, but also upon his being a good man. We shall not linger with these, for none of them lasted, though some of the things they advocated have parallels in the present.

Nevertheless, some groups which emerged in those early years, mainly in the fifth century, have persisted to the present as separate churches. They are relatively small in number and often forgotten by the rest of Christendom. They are, however, important to themselves if not to other Christians, and the presence of some of them in the World Council of Churches is living evidence that they exist. We shall glance at a few.

The Coptic Church is located in Egypt, to which—so tradition says—Christianity was brought by Mark in the first century. Alexandria was a very strong center of Christianity in the early days of the Church, and from it came some of its greatest theologians, among them Clement, Origen, and Athanasius. In the fifth century, as a result of dissenting views on the nature of Christ's divinity, the greater part of the Egyptian Church became separated from Rome and has continued to the present as an independent group. Under great pressure from the Moslems, it has nevertheless kept Christianity alive in that area. Recently the Coptic Church has come into the news from the discovery of some manuscripts in Egypt, published under the title *The Gospel According to Thomas,* which may include some sayings of Jesus not found in the New Testament.

The Mar Thoma Syrian Church of Malabar is in India. Tradition says Christianity was taken to India by Thomas, though a more sober judgment holds that it was established there by missionaries from Persia in the fourth century. In any case it is one of the oldest existing churches. It is called Jacobite from its adoption of the doctrine and liturgy of Jacob of Syria, patriarch of Antioch. One of the six presidents of the World Council of Churches in the 1954-61 period, the Metropolitan Juhanon Mar Thoma, is of this church, as was originally the late distinguished president of Isabella Thoburn College, Sarah Chakko. The active participation of this ancient church, now usually called the Mar Thoma, in the World Council is a vivid reminder of the recency of many of our denominations.

Another very early but still existing church is the Apostolic Armenian. It is the earliest national church, for the king of Armenia was converted to Christianity about the year 300, and he made this the official religion of the state before Constantine. Its people have been terribly persecuted, and Armenia is now under Soviet control.

4. THE EASTERN ORTHODOX CHURCH

Far exceeding in importance any of these divisions was the great schism of 1054 which rent the Church asunder into two great branches of Catholic Christendom, never to the present reunited. The Eastern Orthodox Church, often called the Greek Orthodox from its origins as contrasted with Latin Christianity, consists today of a number of autocephalous (that is, self-headed and independent) churches.[12] Yet it is one church, with the same doctrines, liturgy, and forms of government. It is the dominant church not only in Greece and Russia, but also in most of the satellite countries of the Soviet Union, though in Poland, Czechoslovakia, and part of Yugoslavia the Roman Catholic Church predominates. Unlike the Roman Church, which uses Latin in its masses everywhere, the Eastern worship is in the language of the people. Yet in most respects its forms have varied little since the great division of 1054.

What caused the split? Ostensibly it was because the Western Church wished to add a word, *filioque,* to the already established and authoritative Nicene Creed, making it read, "The Holy Spirit proceeds from the Father and from the Son." On this occasion the patriarch of Constantinople and the pope at Rome excommunicated each other, the patriach denouncing Western errors in doctrine and practice and the pope retaliating by anathematizing his accuser. But as often happens in families where divorces occur, the flare-up was simply the "last straw" when the separation had been going on for a long time.

The real reasons for the split are to be found in "temperamental incompatibility" and rivalries for power. The East had previously been the more theologically minded, and some of the greatest theologians of the early centuries came out of it. The West was more organizational, practical, and legalistic. In the West there was only one major seat of authority, Rome, while in the East there were four, Alexandria, Jerusalem, Antioch,

[12] Officially, but with little direct jurisdiction, the patriarch of Constantinople is the head of the Orthodox churches. There is now a strong rivalry between the patriarchates of Constantinople and of Moscow, each claiming headship over the other autocephalous churches.

and Constantinople. These often quarreled among themselves, particularly Alexandria and Antioch, but were located close enough together to have kindred interests, and as they were jointly weakened by the Moslem advance they tended to pull together and away from Rome. Increasingly they resented domination in their internal affairs by the pope, who claimed authority over them by divine right, and when Pope Nicholas I (d. 867) deposed the patriarch of Constantinople and invalidated his ordination it was a particularly hard pill to swallow. The West made claims for the primacy of the pope which the East repudiated; the East with a sense of superior culture looked down on the Western barbarians. If the split had not taken place over the *filioque,* it certainly would have over something else.

That the Eastern Orthodox Church is today within the ecumenical movement along with Protestants while the Roman Church is not gives evidence of its greater flexibility. Yet it has its own elements of inflexibility. It is equally firm in its adherence to the apostolic succession, to its veneration of the saints and especially the Blessed Virgin, and to its conviction that it, and it alone, is the one true Church. The Church as the Orthodox conceive it is the mystical Body of Christ, the extension within the world of the Incarnation, which is the focal point of their theology, and therefore it is sinless. At ecumenical conferences the Orthodox sometimes feel impelled to introduce separate reports, for to ask the Church to repent is from this point of view like asking Christ to repent.

From its point of view to encourage missions is to encourage proselytism. This has been a point of disagreement in reference to the proposed merger of the World Council of Churches with the International Missionary Council, for according to the Orthodox view the Church is perpetuated not by seeking to enlist new members from outside its fold but by those born into it. This is indicative of its generally self-contained, tradition-centered point of view. As for doctrine, all this was settled at the first seven great ecumenical councils. Hence, this truth must be maintained graciously but firmly against all novelties of interpretation.

What of the place of the laity in this system? We have seen how within the Roman Church the laity became subordinate and the bishops and priests became virtually the Church. Was this situation corrected under Orthodoxy?

In theory, the laity have a larger place in Orthodoxy than in Roman Catholicism. The idea of "sobornost," a sense of spiritual unity which is very central to this system, emphasizes the collective will. It theoretically provides the possibility both of further ecumenical councils, though it has not seemed necessary for centuries to hold them, and of lay participation as an essential part of the Body of Christ. The Church is a sacramental unity of love, and the clergy and laity together make up the *pleroma* (fullness) of the Church. As a consequence of this doctrine, theology is a legitimate province of the layman, and there have been more outstanding lay theologians in Orthodoxy in recent years than in either Roman Catholicism or Protestantism.[13]

There is, however, a counteracting force which keeps the laymen still in a subordinate status. This is the fact that the clergy are the custodians of the Holy Mysteries—that is, the sacraments. These are very basic to Orthodox life and thought, not to reenact the sacrificial death of Christ as in the Roman Mass, but to bring God and man together in a mystical union that gets its meaning from the meeting of divinity with humanity in the Incarnation. The separation, therefore, between clergy and laity is almost equivalent to the distinction between

[13] Stephen Neill points out an ecumenical problem arising from the fact that a majority of Orthodox theologians, especially in Greece, are laymen while according to tradition the prelates alone should pronounce on faith and order. *Brothers of the Faith* (Nashville: Abingdon Press, 1960), p. 78.

sacred and profane, and the laity may not even enter the inner sanctuary of an Orthodox Church.[14]

So, if the laity are really to be reinstated to their initial place in the Church, as comprising Christ's followers without clerical distinctions, we must look elsewhere than to either Roman Catholicism or Eastern Orthodoxy. Does the Reformation, with Luther's watchword of "the priesthood of all believers," provide this approach? We must see in the next chapter.

[14] Kraemer, *op. cit.*, p. 54.

Chapter III

HOW OUR DIVISIONS CAME ABOUT—THE REFORMATION AND SINCE

AGAIN WE HAVE IN THIS CHAPTER THE TASK OF TRYING TO BRING together into brief compass some exceedingly intricate and important historical movements and to suggest how they have left consequences that extend into the present scene. Again, as before, we shall look at these movements from a dual standpoint—to see how they have affected the emergence of denominations, and along the way to note what happened to the laity.

1. PRE-REFORMATION STIRRINGS

A few pages back we saw how the Church, starting from an essentially fluid New Testament fellowship of witness and service, became catholic, then Catholic, ecclesiastical, hierarchical, and authoritative, with a sacramental system of great temporal as well as spiritual power and with the bishop of Rome elevated to a position of supremacy over all as the pope of the Roman Catholic Church. We shall not attempt to trace this history further except to indicate some cracks appearing in its wall of clerical power before the Reformation, and then the major assault and rift connected with the name of Martin Luther.

There were some great ecclesiastics and priest-theologians in the Middle Ages. The names of Anselm, archbishop of Canterbury; of Bernard, the abbot of Clairvaux; and of Thomas Aquinas, superlative Dominican scholar whose *Summa Theologiae* is still authoritative for Roman Catholicism, will endure as long as church history is studied. Yet greatness was not confined to the clergy. The poet Dante, who did much to popularize and through literary channels to perpetuate the theology of medieval orthodoxy, was a layman. So was Francis of Assisi. His order, or "rule," of friars minor received the blessing of the pope and came to have a very important place within the Roman Catholic Church, but in *The Little Flowers of St. Francis* the members of the order are always spoken of as Brother Leo or Brother Elias, never as Father. Since the monasteries, so influential a part of the religious and social history of the medieval period, were composed of both priests and lay brothers, or friars, it is difficult in retrospect to draw a sharp line. Yet the line is very clear between "the religious," whether monks or nuns, who took perpetual vows of poverty, celibacy, and obedience, and those laymen who remained within the world to pursue their ordinary tasks. Something of a similar stratification, with professionally employed laymen in religious vocations as an intermediate stratum, remains implicitly to the present in Protestantism as it does clearly in Roman Catholicism.

What of the stirrings which were pointing the way toward a radical break with Roman Catholic ecclesiastical power, and with it the exclusive status of the priesthood?

Several types of protest appeared before the Reformation and were in a sense forerunners of it. One of these which produced a division that became permanent was led by Peter Waldo, or Valdez, in the twelfth century. Formerly a rich merchant of Lyons, he became convinced that he ought to take literally the injunction, "If you would be perfect, go, sell what you possess and give to the poor, and you will have treasure in heaven; and come, follow me" (Matt. 19:21). Maintaining that the Bible was the sole rule of faith and practice and that he and those of kindred conviction were called by Christ to go about two by two in poverty and fasting, preaching and denouncing current evil practices in the church, Waldo and his followers soon brought upon themselves opposition and excommunication. Undaunted, they continued to preach and established their own ordained ministry, though in the beginning this was entirely a lay movement. The Waldensian Church, small in numbers but a symbol of creative tenacity, still survives in Italy under the shadow of the Vatican and is a member of the World Council of Churches.

A second type of stirring which has left its imprint, though not in a separate denomination, is the mystical piety of the fourteenth century. Led by such thinkers and men of dedicated insight as Meister Eckhart and Johannes Tauler, this movement stayed within the church because it made no open attacks upon it, but put the emphasis, not on sacramental salvation, but on the inner life of the individual. Famous among the writings of this era which have survived to be read today are the anonymous *Theologia Germanica* (German Theology), which greatly influenced Luther; the *Cloud of Unknowing;* and one of the major devotional writings of all times, the *Imitation of Christ.* The last, which bears the name of Thomas à Kempis, was probably originally written at least in considerable part by Gerhard Groote, with à Kempis as copyist and editor making interpolation and additions.[1]

Both Tauler and Groote were very eloquent and devoted preachers who were the leading figures in a religious fellowship who called themselves "Friends of God." This group, centered mainly in Germany and living in the world without monastic vows, was composed of both clergy and laity. Living in sim-

[1] The exact relation of Groote to à Kempis is this literary and spiritual classic has not been finally determined. It bears in some portions a close resemblance to Groote's *Spiritual Diary,* yet its general flavor is that of a cloister, to which à Kempis belonged in the monastery of Mount St. Agnes while Groote was for the most part a traveling evangelist. It should be borne in mind regarding this, as about our Scriptures, that an amalgam of authorship in those days did not constitute the moral and literary offense of plagiarism it does today.

plicity and poverty and devoting themselves not only to preaching, but also to a devotional study of the Scriptures and to deeds of service, they have left behind them a fragrance out of proportion to their numbers. Groote's influence led to the founding in the Netherlands of a similar nonmonastic but more organized communal group called the Brethren of the Common Life, and in one of their schools Thomas à Kempis studied.

Not only has this movement left to us a great literary heritage of devotion, but the existence of such groups six centuries ago points to something of much importance today. Wherever the emphasis is on ecclesiastical structure there is a deep chasm between clergy and laity. Where it is on service, the devotional life, or the study of the Scriptures, clergy and laity work together as the *laos,* the people of God.

A third pre-Reformation type of protest was that of the Englishman John Wyclif and his disciple John Huss of Bohemia (now Czechoslovakia) in the late fourteenth and early fifteenth centuries. Wyclif is now most famous for his translation of the Bible into English, but in his time he was better known for his opposition to the doctrine of transubstantiation, his view of the Church as consisting of God's elect regardless of the sacerdotal institution, and his sending out of unordained "poor priests" as itinerant lay preachers to carry the gospel to the people. Though deprived of his lectureship at Oxford and severely condemned, he had enough intellectual and political standing to die in his bed. His follower John Huss was not so fortunate; he was burned at the stake in 1415. Yet his influence was not lost, for from it came later the *Unitas Fratrum,*[2] the spiritual ancestor of the Moravians who had a great influence upon John Wesley.

Both Wyclif and Huss were priests of the Roman Church and would have preferred to reform it from within, not to

[2] Literally, "Unity of the Brethren" but usually known as United Brethren,

break with it. Yet both saw the laity as well as clergy to be essential to its nature, and one of the prime charges against Huss was that he wanted in the Lord's Supper to give the cup to the laity. The "priesthood of all believers," even before Luther's enunciation of this principle, was inherent in the protest against a hierarchial and priest-centered church.

Yet it remained for Luther to make this principle explicit. We must now turn to the question of how and why he did it and with what results.

2. LUTHER AND THE PRIESTHOOD OF ALL BELIEVERS

In recent years the observance of Reformation Sunday on the last Sunday of October has spread the knowledge that the Reformation dates most precisely from Martin Luther's nailing of his ninety-five theses on the door of the church at Wittenberg on October 31, 1517. Likewise the Martin Luther film has brought considerable concreteness of understanding to many who previously had little knowledge of his life or its central struggles.

Before looking specifically at what Luther did to inaugurate the Reformation it is necessary to outline some of the forces, more influential than any of the particular movements just mentioned, which led up to it. The basic factor was the vast amount of power, not only spiritual, but also political and economic, which the Roman Catholic Church had come to exercise over the people. Much of this power was beneficial in holding Western Europe together in a great social unity and maintaining order in what might otherwise have been far more chaotic times. But with this power came corruption and an undercurrent of unrest.

The church through its sacramental system had the power to determine one's status in the afterlife as well as in this, for it could give absolution for sin or it could excommunicate an offender. As an outgrowth of its system of penance, the sale of indulgences to shorten the period in purgatory for oneself or one's loved ones became a lucrative business. It was this traffic in indulgences, ostensibly to get money to build Saint Peter's Church in Rome but actually to enable an aspiring archbishop to purchase another archbishopric, that touched off the Reformation.

Yet nationalism was also an active factor in the situation. There had been repeated clashes as to whether the pope or the emperor had superior power. Smoldering all the time was the resentment of the German people, whether princes or ordinary laity, at the idea of being dominated from Italy and having to pay taxes to a foreign power. The use of much of this money to put up elaborate buildings elsewhere and increase the holdings of the church did not make them feel more content.

There were also intellectual movements stirring, centering in the Renaissance and the writings of humanists like Erasmus, that challenged the authority of the church in matters of belief and put a new value on the individual human spirit. Philosophical currents were also moving away from the idea of the Church and the State as over-all, transcendent realities to individual churches and particular states—that is, from Platonic realism to nominalism. The times were ripe for change.

We must pass over many events in Luther's personal history and the occurrences of those stormy years. Yet the whole needs to be seen against the backdrop of Luther's experience as an Augustinian monk and teacher of philosophy and theology; his struggle for inner peace, which was unsatisfied until the doctrine of justification by faith emancipated him from a "works" idea of salvation; his revulsion at the corruption of the gospel through the sale of indulgences; his dramatic protest in the ninety-five theses, with the subsequent attacks upon him and his excommunication from the Roman Church; his heroic defense at the risk of his life at the Diet of Worms in

1521; his subsequent "protective custody" through the help of the Elector of Saxony at Wartburg Castle, where he translated the New Testament into German; his writing of great hymns, some of which we still sing; and his creation of new forms of worship in the language of the people. There are other books which tell these events in detail, among the most interesting of which is Roland H. Bainton's *Here I Stand.*[3]

From this standpoint the year 1520 is more crucial than 1517, for in this one year, when he was already under severe condemnation, Luther wrote four important works which epitomize the position to which his previous convictions had been leading him. To summarize these will suggest the movement of his thought in regard to the laity.

In May of that year he put out a little tract entitled *On Good Works.* After defining the noblest of all good works to be "to believe in Christ," he affirmed the essential goodness of ordinary trades and occupations and denounced those who "limit good works so narrowly that they must consist in praying in church, fasting or giving alms."[4] This was a radical break with the idea of the intrinsic superiority of the religious life. It emphasized the sacredness of the common life and the reality of Christian vocation (calling) amid the many vocations of daily life.

In August of the same year Luther issued an epoch-making treatise, *To the Christian Nobility of the German Nation.* In this he declared that three walls by which the Roman Church had defended its power must be overthrown. First, the pretended superiority of religious to ordinary vocations is baseless, since all believers are priests. Second, the pope does not have an exclusive right to interpret the Scriptures, since every believer has the God-given right of private judgment. Third, it is not the pope alone, but also the temporal authorities, who

[3] Nashville: Abingdon Press, 1950.
[4] *Op. cit.*, III.

must try to reform the abuses in the Church. He called for numerous practical reforms, of which the most revolutionary proposal was for the abolition of the celibacy of the clergy.

Two months later he wrote an important treatise on the sacraments. Here he put the emphasis on justification by faith alone, though he believed that the sacraments could be a vehicle of divine grace leading to justification, a form of the proclamation of the Word. He reduced the number of the sacraments from seven to two—baptism and the Lord's Supper, criticized denying the cup to the laity, and substituted consubstantiation for transubstantiation; that is, he affirmed the Real Presence of Christ in both a spiritual and a bodily manner in the Lord's Supper.

The fourth document of that year, put forth in the midst of attacks and the issuance of the papal bull of condemnation, was *On Christian Liberty*. In this he declared that the liberty of the Christian man is derived, not from his works, but from the new life in Christ imparted by divine grace to those justified and forgiven.

Thus it appears that Luther's major contributions were outlined by 1520. Here we find the primary emphases of the Reformation: Justification by faith alone, the authority of the Bible, the right of private judgment in interpreting its message, the priesthood of all believers, the sacredness of the common life. Had these notes continued to be uppermost, the laity could have come into their rightful place as an integral part of the Church, equal in status with the clergy even though ordination might impart special functions to the latter. The gulf between sacred and secular was ready for bridging.

It did not turn out that way, however. Why not?

Before attempting to say why, a further word is in order about the meaning of the "priesthood of all believers." Luther never meant by this phrase that the clergy should cease being clergy and the laymen begin to do the preaching and administer the sacraments. What he did mean by it stems from his idea of the Church as a corporate fellowship of Christian believers, every member of it a sinner, yet every member justified by faith alone, saved by grace alone. In this experience all Christians are priests, for all can approach God through the one Mediator, Jesus Christ, and each can witness to God's saving grace by humble obedience in the duties of his daily life. For some this vocation, or divinely given calling, may be preaching the Word and administering the sacraments; for others it may be laboring in the fields or home or market place. Yet all Christians are equally under God's calling. In short, there is a functional but not an *essential* difference between clergy and laity.

This is a great idea, and a very true one, which the Church is seeking to recover today. Yet it never really took hold even in Luther's day.

Kraemer in *A Theology of the Laity* suggests a number of reasons.[5] One of these is the difference between a "baptized"—or we might add, a nominal Christian whether baptized or not—and a "believing" Christian. Luther's thought centered in the latter. In our present situation of the blending of secularism with church membership, neither a priesthood of the laity nor a sense of divine calling in daily life is apt to be very meaningful.

A second reason why the priesthood of all believers did not take hold was that the laity had so long been kept in a state of spiritual immaturity, dependent on the clergy for their salvation and not understanding much about the Bible or the Christian faith, that they could not suddenly function as spiritual adults. In spite of four hundred years of Protestantism since that time, who would say that this situation is wholly past?

However, the most serious reason of all lay in the doctrine of the nature of the Church. Here contradictory elements caused the priesthood of all believers to bog down.

[5] *Op. cit.*, pp. 63-67.

The Reformation placed great emphasis on the pure preaching of the Word and the right administration of the sacraments as the true marks of the Church. To the present these notes are often stressed as the essence of the Protestant understanding of the Church. Yet who but a theologically educated clergy were capable of such "pure" preaching? And who but the ordained clergy could "rightly" administer the sacraments? If this is what the Church is, the laymen can listen to the preaching and receive the sacraments, but their own priesthood is not evident. Furthermore, the old stratification between a religious calling and the demands of daily life is reinstated.

The right way out of this impasse was not to set untrained and unordained laymen to preaching and serving at the Lord's Table. Luther had pointed the true way in stressing functional differences within the essential equality of all divine callings. If the emphasis had then been placed not so exclusively on preaching and the sacraments but *on witness and service in and to the world* as marks of the true Church, the laity could have found their place of priesthood. The emphasis was not thus placed, however, and the stratification continued.

It still continues, and the same barriers persist. Even before the present emphasis on the laity, occasional attempts have been made to revive the idea in various movements stemming from the Reformation, but in general one may say that the priesthood of all believers was stillborn.

Other history-making forces were at work which must be noted before leaving this brief look at Luther's influence. In spite of his counseling of Christian love, in the Peasants' War he sided with the princes against the peasants and denounced the latter in the most savage terms. This alienated the working-class laity who initially were disposed to accept gladly the new faith. This alienation has cast its shadow into the present, accented less by a particular event of the sixteenth century than by a persistent trend toward social conservatism which was intensified by Luther's emphasis on docile obedience within one's station as the will of God.

A corresponding development is seen with reference to the State. Luther solidified his case for Protestantism by appealing for support to the ruling temporal powers, thus paving the way for a union of nationalism with Protestantism. This was not sheer expediency on his part; it was based on the idea stated in Rom. 13:1 that "there is no authority except from God, and those that exist have been instituted by God." The sphere of Christian justification and calling was in the personal life; the State was God's instrument for taking care of public matters.[6] This dualistic Christian ethic has spread much further than Lutheranism, but came sharply into the scene of world events as recently as World War II, when Lutheran influence in Germany counseled obedience to the ruling powers until Hitler attacked the Church and came to be viewed as Antichrist. In lands not primarily Lutheran, and regardless of the presence of an established church, it must still be noted that the Protestant moral outlook today seldom expresses itself in forms at variance with the edicts of the State.

A third development which has both parallels and direct effects in the present was Luther's break with the humanists and the intellectual leaders of the Renaissance. This does not mean simply a lack of intellectual acumen either in Luther or the theologians who came after him, but rather a redirection of attention from man to God and from mind to heart, with the use of powerful intellects to subordinate reason to revelation. Luther broke with Erasmus primarily over predestination, but a cleavage of interest and a sense of what was important made the break inevitable. And, to the present, not only the

[6] Note, however, that Luther spoke of the obligation of passive disobedience if the ruler acted in a manner contrary to the Word of God. Historically, this has been less accented than the obligation of obedience.

laboring man but the intelligentsia are largely outside the Protestant churches.

This is not to lay at Luther's door all that has happened since his day to make the Church a middle-class institution, in the main both intellectually and socially conservative. Yet the forces set in operation at the genesis of Protestantism are still in operation. As a result, there is often a gap between the theological and social views of seminary-trained clergy and the rank-and-file laity, with an ever-present temptation to maintain the *status quo* instead of the laity's moving forward.

Thus the time is ripe for renewal and reconstruction of the idea of the priesthood of all believers, a projection of the Christian gospel into the whole of life through the witness and service of every Christian. The need in economic, political, and intellectual spheres is perhaps most evident, but it is needed everywhere. That for the most part the preaching and the administration of the sacraments must remain the functions of the clergy is not under challenge, and not to be deplored unless some exclusive emphasis or artificial exaltation of status is attached to these functions. What is to be deplored is the layman's seeing his Christian duty as limited to being a handyman in the institutional structure of the Church, with no awareness that in his daily occupation, his political responsibilities, and his community contacts he *is* the Church within the world.

3. CALVIN AND CALVINISM

More briefly now we must trace what happened in the emergence of the other major families of faith which stem from the Reformation. All were in a sense streams flowing from the great watershed which bears the name of Luther, but with characteristics differing according to both their leaders and their times.

Calvin was a man of very different background and temperament from Luther. Trained originally as a lawyer, he never lost his legalistic bent, but turned all the capacities of a clear and forceful, logically disciplined mind to the disciplining of Geneva and the setting forth of a Protestant theology that centered in the absolute sovereignty of God. His *Institutes of the Christian Religion,* written when he was a young man of twenty-six and subsequently revised several times but never basically changed, still remains one of the major theological classics. He came to Geneva when it was in a chaotic state of transition to acceptance of the new faith and made it into the most thoroughly Protestant and "moral" city of all Christendom. He did not do this without a struggle, but in the struggle some important principles still basic to our political as well as church situation emerged. He was the progenitor of the Presbyterian and Reformed churches of today, and though with subsequent important variations, of Congregationalism as well. A younger contemporary of Luther, he has rightly been given in history a place alongside Luther as architect of the Reformation.

It may surprise some readers to learn that Calvin was a layman. Or was he? In any case, he was never ordained in the usual sense by the laying on of hands, though when he was appointed as preacher in the Geneva church he was introduced to his office without this rite.[7] Furthermore, he was a self-taught theologian with a humanistic and legal but not a seminary training. Nor was he officially a citizen of Geneva until, twenty-three years after he began to guide its destinies, the Council conferred citizenship upon him on Christmas Day of 1559. These are not simply curious facts; they are indications that a layman of dedication and ability can serve Christ and the Church on a level that makes official status seem unimportant.

A word needs to be said about Geneva also before we begin to look at ways in which the Reformed, or Calvinist, wing of the Reformation diverged from the Lutheran. In Germany in

[7] Walker in *A History of the Christian Church,* p. 389, says categorically, "He was never ordained."

Luther's time capitalism had made headway only in the large cities, and Luther's outlook was chiefly in terms of the personal relationships of the farm and small village. He wanted life to be simple and interrelated as each man dutifully kept to his own station in life, and he fought against the corrupting influence of the great financial houses, like the Fuggers, who were the pope's bankers. In Geneva, on the other hand, capitalism had gone much further in replacing the medieval feudal basis of society. Calvin saw that the advance of new economic structures was inevitable, and he conceded to it at the point of sanctioning the taking of interest on loans, which formerly had been banned as usury. Though he by no means created capitalism, he modified and furthered it by giving Christian sanction, not only to the taking of interest, but to the disciplines of hard work, diligence in business, and frugal living by which to save one's money and hence have more to reinvest. This was to have an effect on the economic life of America when Calvinism came to these shores, and in spite of major changes, especially in the twentieth century, the effect has not yet wholly disappeared.[8]

What of Calvin's views on theology and the Church and their influence? They are many-sided but we shall look only at the central ones: the interpretation of the Bible, predestination and election, the relation of the Church to the secular authorities, and the moral duties of the Christian citizen.

Calvin, much more than Luther, equated the Bible with the Word of God. To Luther, the Word is God's assurance of salvation in Christ through justification by faith; the Bible is the channel or medium through which this Word comes to us, but not an inerrant compilation of statements of fact. Hence

[8] The classic work which traces this connection is Max Weber, *The Protestant Ethic and the Spirit of Capitalism* published in Germany in 1905 (New York: Charles Scribner's Sons, 1930). Translated by Talcott Parsons. See also R. H. Tawney, *Religion and the Rise of Capitalism* (New York: Harcourt, Brace & Company, 1926), and Georgia Harkness, *John Calvin: the Man and His Ethics* (Apex ed.; Nashville: Abingdon Press, 1958).

the book of James, which stresses good works instead of faith, Luther called "an epistle of straw." Calvin was much more inflexible. He saw that the Bible must be interpreted and therefore could not always be taken simply at face value. The source of interpretation he found in the Holy Spirit. Yet in practice, it was the interpretation given by the Holy Spirit *to him,* and not to anyone else, that seemed authoritative. Accordingly, the Reformed tradition became more Bible-centered than the Lutheran, and often more literalistic. Foundations were laid for an orthodoxy that was to resist change as the historical approach to the Bible came into common practice, and the Presbyterian Church more than any other in recent times was to be rent by controversy between the fundamentalists and the liberals.

Calvin's doctrine of predestination was a direct outgrowth of his great sense of the sovereign omnipotence of God. He found a biblical basis for it in the writings of Paul, especially in Rom. 8:28-30, but it was congenial to his way of thinking to regard God as the ultimate arbiter of all human destiny. Luther had believed in predestination too, as Augustine long before him had, but they were too soft-hearted to assert a double predestination—that is, election to damnation as well as to salvation. Calvin's stern logic went all the way.

It should be noted, however, that neither Calvin nor the Calvinists ever would say that it was God who made man sin. All are sinners, with the curse of Adam's fall upon us, but when one sins it is his own fault and he must take the consequences. It was this rigorous moral imperative that gave tenacity to the Calvinistic or Puritan virtues, and it was a very important quality in building ruggedness of character not only in Geneva and Puritan England but in New England and America as well. It should be added also that in spite of the apparent inscrutability of the divine will, the believers in predestination found a certain comfort in it which gave an inner security to their living. One need not worry, if one's fate is in God's hands.

It was at the point of the relation of the Church to the secular authorities that Calvin's chief struggles lay. While in the end he established a theocracy—that is, a church-dominated form of public life—this did not happen in a day. In the early years of his ministry at Geneva he and his associate Guillaume Farel were forced out of the city by the civic Council, and he remained in exile for three years until recalled. The issue then was over the manner of the administration of the Lord's Supper, which Calvin rightly thought lay in the province of the Church to decide. As time went on, however, more and more power was given to Calvin and to the body of laymen called the Consistory. It was they who assumed responsibility for toning up the morals of the city, and the Council though sometimes reluctantly supported them in it.

Calvin's organization of the Geneva church with a body of laymen as the Consistory to carry responsibility both in the church and in the community was a very important step. While we should not approve today of all the "blue laws" they sought to enforce, this marked a crucial development in the assumption by laymen of responsibility for both their church and their city. It was the forerunner of all the Consistories, Sessions, Vestries, and Official Boards to the present, with the difference that these latter do not so often think of their Christian duty as extending beyond the confines of the church.

A profound influence has stemmed from Calvinism in matters of education, politics, and economics. Calvin himself believed greatly in the need of education, both for clergy and laity, and the establishment of the University of Geneva in 1559 was a crowning achievement of his career. This same impulse led to the founding of Harvard College in 1636, almost as soon as the Puritans had set foot on New England soil, and to great numbers of Presbyterian colleges throughout America.

New England Congregationalism, with its roots in the Puritan revolution in England and the demand for religious freedom as well as in Calvinistic theology, laid the foundations of American democracy. It was a dominant force not only in the revolt against oppression, but also in the establishment of a representative government on the basis of the equality of all men before God. It was not the only strain that helped to fashion constitutional government in America, but it played no small part in its development.

In the economic sphere the Puritan virtues of hard work, thrift, honesty, sobriety, and chastity gave great reinforcement to an expanding capitalist economy which demanded not only financial and administrative skills but personal discipline. Neither Luther nor Calvin believed that "good works," whether as penance, ordinary morality, or diligence in business could win salvation. Yet Calvin, like Luther, believed that daily work is a sphere of divine calling within which to serve and glorify God. Furthermore, by right living the elect could demonstrate their calling and election. Hence, personal discipline in hard work, frugality, and the curbing of the impulses of the flesh were Christian duties. As time went on, the religious roots of this impulse were largely lost sight of, but the fruits remained. One still sees them both in the glorification of the "self-made man" and in a Protestant emphasis on these virtues, which are now often spoken of disparagingly as "bourgeois morality."

4. THE ANGLICANS

We must take a look now at how some of the other great families in the household of Christian faith developed, how they regard the Church, and what is the place of the laity in them.

The Anglican Church, so called from its being the Church of England, is the mother church of the Protestant Episcopal Church in America and of numerous other Anglican churches in various parts of the world. They are mainly independent, but the Lambeth Conference brings their bishops together once in ten years. All have bishops, for that is what the word "episcopal" means. All have a liturgy and a prayer book derived from the English *Book of Common Prayer* though not always identical with it. All are in intercommunion with each other, that is, they recognize the validity of each other's sacraments and can take Communion together. A word about their origin must suffice.

Everybody knows the story of Henry VIII and his six wives and of how he broke with the pope when he wanted to divorce his first wife, Catherine of Aragon, because she bore him no son for a successor. This was a crucial event, but by no means the sole cause of the break. England had quite different interests from Italy, which then seemed a long way off, and wanted to be independent of foreign control in religious as in political matters. Henry VIII, with all of his unpleasant qualities, was a strong ruler and saw an opportunity both to exalt his own power and to weld England together into a centralized government by making himself the head of the Church. His ruthless destruction of the monasteries and his beheading of Sir Thomas More and others who opposed him were steps in this direction. But he was shrewd enough not to make many changes in liturgy or doctrine. Thus was inaugurated the linkage of Church and State which makes Queen Elizabeth II today the head of the Church of England and gives her the title of "defender of the faith." [9]

Aside from the establishment of a national Church of England by breaking with the papacy, the only important change at first was the placing of the Bible in English in the churches, chained there for safekeeping. This was done through the agency of Archbishop Cranmer, who in the reign of Henry's son Edward VI [10] forged two more links in Anglicanism by

[9] While she is the titular head, the Archbishop of Canterbury is the acting ecclesiastical head.

[10] A boy king who reigned only from the age of ten until his death at sixteen. The real ruler was his uncle who acted as regent.

compiling the *Book of Common Prayer* and the Forty-two (later Thirty-nine) Articles of Religion. These represent both a fuller formulation of Protestant thought and a conservative richness and depth which have helped to keep this church steady through the centuries.

During the long reign of Queen Elizabeth I Protestantism became firmly established, more through compromise for the sake of peace than through strong conviction. It was in this period and the ensuing reign of the Stuart kings that Puritanism became an active challenge to the Established Church. This was to have important consequences, not only in the extension of Calvinism to Great Britain and eventually to the New World, but also in forging changes within Anglicanism.

A primary characteristic of Anglicanism is the fact that it is both Catholic and Protestant, with wide variations within its membership as to which of these elements is stressed. Those who emphasize its Catholic nature attach great importance to the apostolic succession, by which the historic episcopate is thought to be derived in unbroken line from the first apostles, and they make the ordination by a bishop in this succession so essential that outside it there is no true ministry or valid administration of the sacraments. Those adhering most rigidly to this point of view are called Anglo-Catholics, or "high church," and they regard it as a sacrilege to partake of the Lord's Supper from the hands of a person not thus ordained. Other Anglicans and Episcopalians, often referred to as "low church," believe that the episcopacy is a right and proper form of church government, with its historic element emphasizing a great tradition, but they do not deny the validity of other forms of ministry and will take Communion with other Christians to the degree that they feel their canon law permits.

This difference becomes apparent at every ecumenical conference. It is often a source of difference in degrees of cooperation with other Protestant churches. Yet this dual Catholic-

Protestant emphasis is also one of the strong points of Anglicanism, making it a *via media* between opposing patterns of church life. At the same time, the apostolic succession is the main reason why "the ministry and the sacraments" is the most knotty problem in current ecumenical discussion, overshadowing the attention that ought to be given to the total ministry of the Church.

What of the laity in all this? Not much is said about them in histories of Anglican or Episcopal thought. All are expected to be regular worshipers and communicants; some to be vestrymen in charge of the business affairs of the congregation. Lay participation in legislative assemblies, extensive in America, varies from country to country. There is here no such potential for accenting the importance of the laity as in the idea of "the priesthood of all believers." Wherever the hierarchical structure of the Church persists there seems to be a tendency for laymen to assume their traditional, though not their scriptural, role as adjuncts to the clergy.

5. THE FREE CHURCHES

We have now traced the emergence of the three major expressions of the Protestant spirit which have persisted to the present. There are, however, important and in some cases very large Protestant churches which are neither Lutheran nor Reformed nor Anglican. They are so numerous and diverse that we can here only glance at a few of the most familiar.

These churches include Baptists, Congregationalists, Methodists, Disciples, Quakers, Unitarians, and a great many of the smaller sects. Sometimes these are grouped together and called the free churches, sometimes the "gathered community" type of church. Neither term is a very good one. "Free church" is ambiguous, for it can also mean the churches in a country where there is no State church. In the ecclesiastical sense it means negatively "free from bishops in the apostolic succession," but its more positive meaning is greater freedom as to forms of church government, the basis of ordination, and the validity of the sacraments. Thus it is mainly not a matter of the political situation, but of the polity of the church. In matters of ecclesiastical order through representative government the Presbyterian and Reformed are also free churches, while some Lutheran churches do and others do not have bishops. But if we abandon this term for the "gathered" type of church, which stresses free and voluntary membership with much local autonomy in forms of government, we run into so many variations that this is not a very good term either. Perhaps the best we can do is to say that some churches have bishops believed to derive their authority from the apostolic succession while others do not, and the latter for the sake of convenience are usually called free churches.

The earliest of these groups to emerge after the Reformation was the Congregationalists, in seventeenth century England called Independents. They believed that churches should be governed neither by bishops nor by presbyteries, but by each local congregation. Their independence of spirit and insistence on religious freedom in forms of worship brought them under severe persecution as nonconformists, sending them first to Holland and then to New England as the Pilgrim Fathers. Their theology was then mainly Calvinist but the emphasis on religious freedom within a voluntary fellowship made for a flexibility which has enabled modern Congregationalism—now merged in the United Church of Christ—to be essentially liberal and undogmatic in its outlook.

The Baptist church has its roots in the Anabaptist (rebaptiser) movement which in the early days of the Reformation was much persecuted for insisting on adult baptism, the complete separation of Church and State, and the refusal to go to war and to take oaths as being contrary to the word of Jesus. The latter elements were eventually dropped, continuing in the branch that came to be known as Mennonites, but the

Baptist insistence on adult baptism by immersion, the independence of Church and State, and the autonomy of the local congregation have persisted to the present. Although allied with the Congregationalists in England, they separated over adult baptism. It is ironic that when both groups came to America, the New England Congregationalists drove out Roger Williams and the Baptists as heretics, and they took refuge in Rhode Island. Both the Congregationalists and the Baptists have had great missionary zeal, and the fruits of their efforts are to be found all over the world.

A third group which emerged in mid-seventeenth century England as a protest against both the Anglicans and the Puritans was the Quakers, or Society of Friends. Led by George Fox, the Quakers rejected all outward forms of worship, including the sacraments, as too conventional and substituted the leading of the "Inner Light." In the complete equality of all Christians before God there could be no ordained ministry; in Quaker services women as well as men might speak at the leading of the Spirit. Like the Anabaptists the Quakers objected to oaths and to war, and the pacifism of the Quakers with a corresponding concern for the relief of suffering is today a well-known fact. The Quaker fellowship, wholly consisting of laymen in principle though some Quaker churches today have paid ministers, is the most democratic of all the churches. Small in numbers, the Society of Friends has exerted an influence far beyond its numerical proportion in service to society, and is a continuous wholesome reminder in the ecumenical movement that Christian fellowship is essentially a matter of spirit rather than institutional structure.

Then in the eighteenth century came the Methodists. John Wesley was the son of an Anglican clergyman and was himself ordained in this church, remaining in this relation throughout his life. Yet failing to find in it that the deeper needs of his soul were met, he was influenced by some Moravian friends to attend a meeting in Aldersgate Street on May 24, 1738. As he listened to the reading of Luther's Commentary on the Epistle to the Romans his heart was "strangely warmed," and thereafter he became a flaming evangelist for personal redemption through the grace of God. Riding horseback thousands of miles each year to hold meetings under the most difficult circumstances, he did an enormous amount to revive the then sterile religious life of England. Debarred from preaching in the churches, he preached in the fields, around the coal mines, and in the jails. Methodist societies and conferences were formed, with "class meetings" of small groups for mutual support and with considerable use of lay preachers.

There was no official break with the Church of England during Wesley's lifetime; this occurred soon after his death in 1791. From the standpoint of American Methodism the crucial year was 1784 when Wesley, though not himself a bishop, ordained Thomas Coke as one and appointed him to have charge of the work in America, ordaining other men as the need arose. This interrupted the apostolic succession, and the bishops of the Methodist Church are therefore simply chief pastors and administrative officers, theoretically of equal status with every other minister. This church combines in an unusual way the episcopal form of government with the presbyterial by its equal representation of clergy and laymen in the Annual and General Conferences. While it does not have the local autonomy of the Congregational and Baptist churches, it still has a strong local church emphasis in the responsibility placed upon its lay members through its commissions, committees, and the Official Board. This form of organization is a major source of strength as it enlists its ten million members—the largest Protestant group in America—to carry out the decisions of each quadrennial General Conference.

The Disciples otherwise known as the Christian Church is a relatively small but an influential branch of the free churches.

Founded by Thomas and his son Alexander Campbell in the early nineteenth century as an American offshoot from Scottish Presbyterianism, it originally aimed to eschew all denominational divisions by being simply a brotherhood in Christ based on the Bible and emulating the spirit of the first century disciples. Hence, its inclusive name. However, it was destined to become another denomination. Save for fixed practices of adult baptism by immersion and participation in the Lord's Supper at every Sunday service of worship, it is relatively free in its polity and procedures. Much autonomy is given to each local congregation. Laymen have a degree of recognition here not found elsewhere, for not only do laymen customarily participate with the minister in the administering of the sacrament, but have the authority to administer it in their own right.

Here we must stop. To tell the story of the emergence of the other denominations would extend this chapter to the length of a book. Theological differences are not the only cause of division—witness the fact that the Methodist Church was divided over the race question for almost a hundred years until 1939, and there are still unsolved issues in regard to it. Locally if not nationally, differences in educational level or economic status cause divisions, and cutting across denominational lines there are frequent clashes between those of conservative and of liberal outlook. As a result, co-operation between some churches seems relatively easy; in other cases, almost if not quite impossible.

It is obvious that there is plenty of work yet to do before the Body of Christ is one. In the healing of these divisions both laity and clergy must take an active part. The first step is to understand how and why the divisions came about. If this chapter and the preceding one have contributed somewhat to this understanding, they will have fulfilled their function.

Chapter IV

WHAT IS A CHURCH FOR?

In the first chapter we dealt in a general way with the functions of a church in a survey of the various meanings of the word—terms that suggest what the Church is. We saw that in spite of the many divisions within it the Church of Christ is a world-embracing fellowship of those who acknowledge Jesus Christ as Lord and seek to be His followers. The next two chapters traced in outline form how the major divisions came about and at the same time indicated the changing status of the laity in these historical developments. We are ready now to inquire more precisely as to the functions of a church and the place of the laity in their fulfillment.

Note that we say "a church," with a small "c." This does not mean that we have wholly left behind "the Church" written with a capital letter, the inclusive fellowship which embraces within it many thousands of individual churches. Yet from now on we must put the emphasis on the particular rather than the general, for it is in particular local churches that laymen find their most immediate connection with the Church. When we speak of such churches, unless some other designation is called for, we shall mean local congregations more or less related to one another in denominations and all together constituting the visible Church of Christ within the world.

Before looking at particular functions the churches of a community seek to exercise, we must emphasize a basic fact. The Church is first of all a fellowship of Christians; it is secondarily an institution of society. In the first sense it is a distinctive community; there is nothing just like it anywhere else on earth; it has a particular work to do, a calling to fulfill. In the second sense it has much in common with other social institutions. It has rules and regulations; it has representative officials, usually called trustees, who can act for it as a legal entity; it employs and pays a staff, whether ministerial or lay; it invests funds if it has a surplus, borrows at the bank if it lacks them. It brings people together for social occasions, when entertainment or edification or simply the enjoyment of one another's company is the object; it engages in many good works not unlike those sponsored by the community chest or service clubs or the public schools of the community. These institutional aspects of a church are for the most part necessary, and in spite of the perversions to which all sinful humanity is subject, they are for the most part good. Yet they are not primary, and their badness when this occurs stems mainly from what is rightfully secondary being made primary.

As a fellowship of the followers of Christ, a church has one overarching function which transcends all others, and every particular function finds its criterion of usefulness in relation to it. The Church exists to be the carrier of the gospel of Christ; a church is, or it is not, in a full sense a church to the degree that its members are faithful to this mission. When it fails in this the people may meet in ever so grand and impressive a church building, they may have ever so good a time in each other's company, they may do ever so many fine things that are worth doing, but they are not really a church. Instead, they are a social gathering of congenial and usually rather nice people who for reasons of family connection or habit or the following of prevailing pattern—or even the hope of prestige as a factor in economic success—decide to stay with or unite with a church.

To be the carrier of the gospel of Christ is a many-sided task. Is there no more specific way to state it? It takes many forms, at some of which we shall be looking presently. Yet as a guidepost and directive we cannot do better than to take seriously what our Lord said are the two great commandments.

As part of a long and careful research study of theological education there was published in 1956 an important book by H. Richard Niebuhr in collaboration with Daniel Day Williams and James Gustafson entitled *The Purpose of the Church and Its Ministry*. In this the ultimate goal of the Church and its ministry is declared to be the increase of the love of God and neighbor. Expand the term "ministry" to cover the service of the laity as well as clergy and it still remains true that the basic reason why a church exists is to carry forward in the world the gospel of Christ by the increase of the love of God and neighbor.

Since this statement by Niebuhr has now become almost classic it merits quotation at some length:

> Is not the result of all these debates . . . that no substitute can be found for the definition of the goal of the Church as *the increase among men of the love of God and neighbor?* The terms vary; now the symbolic phrase is reconciliation to God and man, now increase of gratitude for the forgiveness of sin, now the realization of the kingdom or the coming of the Spirit, now the acceptance of the gospel. But the simple language of Jesus Christ himself furnishes to most Christians the most intelligible key to his own purpose and to that of the community gathered around him. If the increase among men of love of God and neighbor is the ultimate objective may it not be that many of our confusions and conflicts in churches . . . are due to failure to keep this goal in view while we are busy in the pursuit of proximate ends that are indeed important, but which set us at cross-purposes when followed without adequate reference to the final good? [1]

This task of the Church has many facets as it seeks to relate

[1] New York: Harper & Brothers, pp. 31-32. Used by permission. Niebuhr insists further that "the Church . . . loses its character as Church when it concentrates on itself, worships itself and seeks to make love of Church the first commandment." P. 30.

the gospel both to the ever-recurring needs of humanity and to the particular duties and demands of today's world. God has provided many instrumentalities and agencies, many "means of grace," if we may extend this term beyond its traditional connotation of the sacraments. In short, as the late Archbishop William Temple graphically declared, we live in a sacramental universe.[2] There is little, perhaps potentially nothing, in this universe of men and things that cannot be used to the glory of God and the service of men if Christians have the will and wisdom to turn what is evil to good and to use what is already good to serve these ends. To do so is to be carriers of the gospel of Christ and true members of Christ's Church.

Before we look further at the particular functions of a church, some warnings which have already been hinted at need to be sounded. Since churches must claim from their members time, attention, and both moral and financial support, there is a constant temptation in the competitive struggle with other social institutions to imitate their procedures and thus become secular clubs. In the devotion that is elicited there is a temptation, as Niebuhr puts it, for the Church to worship itself and seek to make the love of Church the first commandment. Yet even when the gospel is ostensibly primary, there is still the danger of too limited a piety. The Church exists to carry the evangel but this is not to say that its sole function is evangelistic in the narrower sense—that is, to make converts. This indeed it needs to do, but it must also build people up in the Christian life and instruct them in the Christian faith. Such instruction ought to extend not only to the church school, but to the pulpit, the woman's society, the men's club, and to every agency of family life. The laity need to be instructed, but they need also to instruct.

In this educative process, a church should lead its members

[2] *Nature, Man and God* (New York: The Macmillan Company, 1934), Ch. XIX.

to be concerned about forms of social evil and injustice both in the local community and in the world and should prompt them to speak, vote, and otherwise act for a better society. This does not, however, mean that a church is simply a reform agency; its political influence and social action must spring from Christian roots and rest on Christian foundations.

Recoiling from the social gospel, some would say that a church has as its sole function the ministry to the inner life and the imparting of divine grace through its sacred rites. Yet this too can run into the "dead end street" of personal indulgence, conformity to conventional patterns, and indifference to great areas of human need.

Whichever way we turn, the business of a church is to be the carrier of the gospel and a mediator of divine grace. But it cannot do this through one channel only. So, what are these particular channels? And what are their pitfalls and possibilities? And how do laymen fit into these functions?

1. CORPORATE WORSHIP

The main reason for having a church building is to provide an appropriate setting for the corporate worship of God in the way of Christ. As was indicated in Chapter I, the architecture ought to be directed to this end, and there is a meaning in the spire, the cross, the chancel, the altar, the pulpit, the lectern, the pews, the hymnbooks, the organ, the choir, and all the other furnishings and symbolism of a sanctuary that should mark it as more than just an ordinary meeting place. The primary function of any church within the inclusive function of being the carrier of the gospel of Christ is to unite the congregation in meaningful, God-serving corporate worship.

The term "God-serving" is used designedly, for a Christian congregation unites in a "service" of worship, not primarily to serve themselves and go away feeling better after "getting a lift," but to serve and honor God. This by no means excludes the call to the service of men which, beginning at the house of worship, should extend through the laity out into the daily life of the people. Yet it is quite different from worship as a psychological exercise, the inducing of a meditative mood for a pleasant feeling of well-being. The Greek word *leitourgia,* from which the word liturgy is derived, though it can be applied to any corporate service of worship, is itself derived from words which mean "public work." [3] Not only does this suggest that to worship God is a form of service, but the word for "public" suggests that the whole people of God, minister and laity alike, are to do something about it.

This raises the question of whether the layman's work in the service of worship is, or ought to be, the same as the preacher's. Certainly, if the priesthood of all believers is taken seriously, both ought equally to serve and honor God. But let us remember that Luther never meant by this term that all Christians must do the same kind of work. What he emphasized was the *essential equality* of all Christian believers, not *identity of function* in types of service.

It is right and proper that the main responsibility for conducting the service of worship should lie with the minister. It is a high art, requiring spiritual depth and sensitivity, biblical knowledge and skills in reading and interpreting the Bible, an intelligent grasp of our Christian faith and heritage, a sense of dignity and fitness, and relevance in the application of a timeless gospel to temporal needs. There have been some great lay preachers in the past, from Peter Waldo to Dwight L. Moody, and there is a place today for occasional lay preaching. But there is sufficient reason why it is not the usual practice. Usually the minister or priest, equipped by long training as well as by spiritual dedication, can preach better, and it is his responsibility.

[3] From *leitos,* public, which is a variant of *laos* and *ergon,* work.

Every minister should consider it his *main* responsibility. A minister as pastor, counselor, administrator, and public servant has, of course, many other things to do, but shame on him if he becomes casual about his conducting of corporate worship on Sunday morning! This, I repeat, is his main responsibility, his primary "public work." If he does it with depth of devotion to the glory of God and the service of men, the chances are that he can meet the other demands upon him with reasonable success; if he is sloppy at this point it is more than likely that he will slip elsewhere as well.

Yet the *laos* have their part also in this "public work," this service to God. It was noted in the previous chapter that when in the post-Reformation Church the pure preaching of the Word and the right administration of the sacraments became the dominant notes by which to define the true Church, the priesthood of all believers slipped out of the picture. It needs to be recovered, but would the turning of these functions over to the laity on a mutual basis restore it?

Whether a layman should preach is largely a matter of fitness. In the matter of the sacraments, however, deep questions of authority are involved; these stem from differing views as to what constitutes the true nature of the Church. From the standpoint of the churches centered in the apostolic succession, it would seem utterly blasphemous for a layman to celebrate the Lord's Supper, though in the Roman Catholic Church baptism in emergencies may be administered by a layman if the right formula is used. From a free-church standpoint the answer is more difficult. Theoretically in the free churches ministers and laymen are equals; functionally there are differences. The most logically consistent of the free churches is the Disciples, whose practice it is in the weekly Communion service, the heart of the Sunday morning service of worship, to have minister and laymen share alike in giving the sacrament to the people.

At this point it is well to be guided by Paul's word, "All

things are lawful unto me, but all things are not expedient" (I Cor. 6:12 K.J.V.). In the early church sermons were preached, baptisms took place, and the agape love feast was presided over as well as participated in before there was an ordained clergy or a sacerdotal institution. But we cannot erase history as if it had never happened. For centuries the celebration of the Lord's Supper has been the function of the priesthood, and today in the free churches, as well as in others, words like these are spoken in the service of ordination: "Take thou authority as an elder in the Church to preach the Word of God, and to administer the holy Sacraments in the congregation." [4] Nothing is to be gained in this matter by flouting history and long tradition. The particular practice and polity of one's denomination had better be observed unless there is some clear reason to challenge it.

Not many laymen care to challenge it, for their work lies elsewhere. Yet how far the possibilities of their work extend is not so commonly recognized.

Everybody recognizes that it is the laymen's job to pay the preacher. At least, every layman *should* recognize it! In this act lies both a high potential of service and a subtle danger. An evidence of the sincerity of Christian conviction in the early church is that they shared not only their prayers and praises but what was in their purses. (See Acts 2:44; 4:34.) While no such complete communalism of possessions is called for today, the principle of stewardship of possessions has not been abrogated. The danger, however, is twofold; first, that economic leverage from the pews may stifle prophetic utterance from the pulpit, and second, and more insidious, that the layman who pays generously may think he has done all that is required.

It is also recognized that among the types of service contributing to the service of corporate worship, some lay persons

[4] Methodist *Discipline* of 1960, ¶ 1921.

will usher, some will sing in the choir, some—usually women—will arrange the flowers on the altar and serve as communion stewards when the sacrament is celebrated. If the roof leaks or the parking lot needs attention, laymen of good conscience on the building and grounds committee will see a responsibility awaiting them without having to be reminded of it by the minister. Even the janitor or sexton, though he is seldom sufficiently appreciated, can make his contribution to the glory of God, and ought not to be expected to do so in lieu of a normal wage. The same holds true of the often overburdened, manifold-dutied church secretary.

What of the layman's contribution to the service of corporate worship in areas below the obvious? Here the opportunities are more intangible, but equally important. We shall speak of but three, obvious enough in words, but more costing in execution.

The first of these is *regularity of attendance*—not attendance when the weather is just right, or when the golfing or gardening possibilities are not so good, or when there are no particular jobs to be done around the house, but attendance every Sunday, rain or shine, in busy times or slack times, with a stimulating minister or a boring one! There are, of course, illness or exceptional legitimate demands to justify an occasional absence. Yet the health or sickness of a church depends to a very large extent on the regularity and fidelity of its members in attendance at the Sunday service of worship. It is the sense of compulsion to attend every Sunday which largely accounts for the strength of the Roman Catholic Church in each local community, and the inner compulsion of the Protestant ought not to be less potent. When one joins a church he joins *the Church,* and not the particular minister or group of people who are to be found there. An intermittent, come-and-go congregation of people who attend church only when they feel like it, or only when they like the minister, is seldom a strong church devoted to the service of God and the enhancement of human good.

A second factor—term it opportunity or requirement as you will—is *active congregational participation.* It has become the mood of the day to look on at most things that can be watched, whether sports, movies, television, or the doings of other people. The vogue of illustrated travelogues probably stems from the fact that one thus gets the illusion of looking in on unfamiliar scenes and cultures, and with so little effort. A similar passivity and mood of spectatorship pervades many, if not most, services of corporate worship. The minister works, the choir works, the ushers work; the people sit decorously, sing or read perfunctorily, repeat the Lord's Prayer with their reflexes, and if the truth be spoken, let their minds go wool-gathering more than they would often publicly admit! The Holy Spirit can pierce many barriers, but one may wonder if such polite passivity is not one of the most impregnable.

This attitude of active participation reveals itself in the way one sings, reads, joins in the spoken prayers or listens responsively, and intangibly but unmistakably in one's total receptive alertness. It makes a great difference not only to the worshiper himself and by the contagion of personality to the rest of the congregation, but also to the minister. Much has been done in recent years through the liturgical movement and instruction in the seminaries to enrich the conduct of public worship. A "deadpan" apathy on the part of the congregation, however, can be a fatal barrier to anything happening beyond the perfunctory rote.

A third requirement and opportunity lies in the *atmosphere of friendly fellowship* which the layman—and perhaps most readily the lay woman—can create or destroy. Warmth of fellowship in a church does not call simply for jocularity or an artificial folksiness; Christian "togetherness" is fellowship in Christ. Yet warmth of fellowship is essential to the enrichment of corporate worship. If a stranger, a person newly come to the community, a foreign student, a person of a minority race, attends a service of worship and finds there no welcome but instead the barrenness of impersonality which pervades so much of contemporary life, he will not soon come again. The tragedy of it is intensified by the fact that unless he has a deep-rooted Christian past, neither will he try any other church next Sunday.

We have dwelt at length on the service of corporate worship and the layman's place in it because this is the primary element in the life of a church. The church has other functions, however, and we must now look at these.

2. THE MEDIATION OF GRACE THROUGH THE SACRAMENTS

From this point on, no attempt will be made to rank the various functions of a church in order of importance. All are so important that one can hardly be said to be inferior to another; all are intertwined; all come to focus in the over-all responsibility of being a carrier of the gospel of Christ. The service of corporate worship is vitally related to every other aspect of the services of the Church of which we shall now speak, and these ramify out from it wherever a church most effectively serves its members and the world.

Largely for the sake of a logical sequence, since the preaching of the word and the administering of the sacraments have long been viewed as the primary marks of the Church, we shall now look further at the second of these functions. It should be clear, however, that this is no more important than other services to be noted later. Without these other services the sacraments can become barren, perfunctory, and unfruitful.

At the heart of the service of corporate worship are these sacred, symbolic acts, seven in number in the Roman Catholic Church and in Eastern Orthodxy, two in normative Protestantism. In addition to baptism and the Lord's Supper in the Roman Church the other five are confirmation, holy orders, matrimony, penance, and extreme unction. The Anglican Church usually regards the first three of these as sacramental rites, and the Anglo-Catholic wing of Anglicanism accepts all seven. The limits of space make it necessary to speak here only of the two which almost all churches have, the principal exceptions being the Quakers and the Salvation Army, who have only spiritual and not external sacramental acts.

We spoke earlier of the sacraments as the time-honored means of grace, though not the sole means. Channels of grace they ought ever to be. Though the clergy must ordinarily administer them, it depends on the laymen who receive them to receive also the grace they are intended to impart. Unless the emphasis is to be placed on the Church as an institution mediating grace inevitably if not automatically through its sacerdotal structure, a great deal of responsibility rests on the recipient. Even in the Roman Catholic Church confession must precede communion in order that the sanctifying grace mediated by the priest may fall on a repentant soul.

Baptism, whether of infants or adults, ought to be more than a social custom or an empty formula. Though attention to detail fitting to the solemnity of the occasion is in order, there is something out of place in undue attention to the baby's christening attire, behavior, or "sweetness." When parents take vows to bring up their children in a Christian family "in the nurture and admonition of the Lord," or when adults take baptismal vows as a public acknowledgment of the desire to lead a Christian life in the fellowship of Christ's followers, these occasions ought to be high and holy moments of deep spiritual import. Something is wrong with the attitude of the person taking these vows if that day does not stand out, as he looks backward on it, as a high day of solemn and joyous memory.

Baptism normally and rightly occurs only once in each Christian's life; the Lord's Supper is a periodic occasion of inner refreshment. The words of invitation in the *Book of Common Prayer,* taken over in the Methodist ritual and in some others, express so perfectly what is required and offered by the Communion service to the inner life of the Christian that they may well be termed not only historic but inspired words. Note them:

> Ye who do truly and earnestly repent you of your sins, and are in love and charity with your neighbours, and intend to lead a new life, following the commandments of God, and walking from henceforth in his holy ways; Draw near with faith, and take this holy Sacrament to your comfort; and make your humble confession to Almighty God, devoutly kneeling.

Repentance, love for one's neighbor, new resolution, moral obedience to God's commandments—these are the demands. Faith, comfort, forgiveness—these are the promises. Is it any wonder that through the centuries the partaking of this sacrament has not only knit Christians together but has brought inner peace to millions?

Yet if this inner peace is to be a present fact and a continuing experience, something more than an occasional sacramental act is needed. We shall look now at a service of the Church which some would consider paramount and which certainly ought never to be neglected. This is the ministry to the inner lives of persons, most readily recognized under the term "pastoral care," but not limited to pastors. An older term, "the cure of souls," suggests the healing which lies at the bottom of it.

3. THE MINISTRY TO THE INNER LIFE

In the midst of even the most opulent and outwardly comfortable society, there is a tremendous burden of inner unrest. This takes manifold forms, of which anxiety, resentment, loneliness, despair, lack of purpose, the battle with temptations whether of the flesh or spirit, and a resulting weight of guilt are the most prevalent. Sometimes these negative attitudes all seem to converge in a single personality to rend and distort it in a way that makes the demon-possession of the New Testament records seem very contemporary. Again one of these factors may overshadow all the rest to dominate one's life. Various attempts have been made to trace personality disturbance to a key source, such as to sexual impulse (Freud), to anxiety (Sullivan, Horney, and much contemporary neo-orthodoxy), to estrangement and alienation (Tillich), or simply to sin (the main stream of the Christian tradition). Sometimes these disturbances are clearly the result of one's own misuse of the freedom God has endowed us with—in short, one's own fault. To some degree this is true of every man, and in this event a sense of guilt, with an awareness both of the need of repentance and of the possibility of divine forgiveness, is far more healthy and curative than any glossing over of the reality of one's sin. Yet again, and frequently, the primary cause of such inner unrest can be traced to a bad social situation, particularly the feeling of being unwanted and unloved; to the lack of inner ideals which give meaning and purpose to life; to a serious illness; to a deep disappointment; to the loss of a loved one by death or default; or to some other circumstance in which a call to repentance simply misses the mark.

What is the function of a church in this complex situation? Clearly, a minister needs to have a basic knowledge of human personality in its development, dynamics, and potential distortions in order to minister to his people. He ought to know both how to counsel fruitfully himself and when to recommend professional psychiatry. Fortunately, there seems to be a better understanding and closer convergence than formerly between the clergy and the psychiatrists, though there are still gaps to be bridged. This is particularly true at the point of the tendency of the later to rule out sin as a nonscientific concept and hence to bypass the basic therapy of repentance and a sense of divine forgiveness, while some ministers, though a diminishing number, fail to recognize that sin cannot be made a catchall to cover every form of evil such as alcoholism and juvenile delinquency.

At this point, as at every other, the service of corporate worship becomes very relevant. It was earlier stated that one ought not to go to church simply to get a lift and to feel better, but rather as an act of worship directed to the glory and service of God. It is no contradiction of this to say that a very important part of the service of God, for which both minister and laity are responsible, is a ministry to the inner lives of persons. To try to use God for psychic benefits is more nearly the mood of magic than religion; to feel cleansed, forgiven, empowered, directed, and lifted to new heights of personal mastery and effective living ought to be the fruit of divine worship. If this does not result, something is wrong either with the way the service is conducted or with the response of the people to it.

We have spoken of the sacraments as particular channels of grace within the service of the corporate worship and shall speak presently of the agencies of evangelism by which people can be won to Christ and His Church. Yet the sacraments are not likely to be very meaningful, and efforts to secure Christian commitments are not likely to reach very deep, unless interpersonal relations are fruitful and good. In such contact of life with life, laymen have a very large part. So, what is the layman's place in this ministry to the needs of the spirit?

An intangible but far-reaching obligation rests upon every Christian. This is the obligation to be understanding, sympathetic, friendly, and helpful in every available way to those caught in life's inner tensions. This is true whether such persons are within or outside the membership of a church. It is true whether one is a highly skilled psychiatrist or professional counselor or simply a Christian who loves people. The love of God and neighbor is best mediated by those loving enough to demonstrate—humbly, tactfully, but steadfastly—that they care about the hurts, the anxieties, and the problems of others. This is true even when firmness in love causes pain. The hardest wall of outer complacency and self-righteousness can be cracked by such deep-going friendliness when nothing else will breach it. This is to say that it is not simply the professional job of the minister, but also the personal responsibility of every Christian, to demonstrate love in action.

A second vitally important channel for the mediation of personal power is through the devotional life engaged in privately, in family worship, or in small groups of those who care enough to meet regularly for collective yet personal prayer. Regarding personal devotions and the family altar, the Church has long recognized and given at least lip service to their importance but has seldom given sufficiently relevant and realistic instruction as to how these are to be maintained. Particularly in this modern day, in the midst of the hurry, overstimulation, and split-apartness of contemporary life, it becomes increasingly difficult to observe "the quiet hour." Yet difficulty does not justify negligence. Fortunately, an increasing number of excellent books and devotional manuals lend help in this field.[5]

More important than the availability of such devotional helps, with the Bible as paramount, is the will to use them. For this there is no substitute. There is no way of knowing statistically how many laymen habitually and frequently engage in personal and family prayer, but from such evidence as we have one may

[5] The devotional literature of the ages yields rich treasures. Among the best modern books on the devotional life are George Buttrick's *Prayer* (Nashville: Abingdon Press, 1942), John Casteel's *Rediscovering Prayer* (New York: Association Press, 1955); Albert Day's *An Autobiography of Prayer* (New York: Harper & Brothers, 1952); Lynn Radcliffe's *Making Prayer Real* (Nashville: Abingdon Press, 1952). My own *Prayer and the Common Life* (Nashville: Abingdon Press, 1948) also deals with this subject at greater length than is here possible.

guess that it is not a very common practice. This in itself is both a symptom and a cause of the tension of our times.

The practice of united worship and mutual sharing of experience in small, informal groups has long been in the tradition of the Church, going back to the Twelve in the upper room and "the church in your house" referred to by Paul (Philem. 2). It is found in the class meetings of early Methodism and in the "cottage prayer meetings"—though usually with a specific evangelistic focus—that were fairly common a generation or two ago. In more recent years the idea has been revived and adapted to the contemporary world through cell groups, spiritual retreats, and units of semiorganized movements such as the Order of the Yoke (D. Elton Trueblood) and the Disciplined Order of Christ (Albert E. Day). The Camps Farthest Out (Glenn Clark) and the ashrams of E. Stanley Jones bring groups together periodically for spiritual fellowship and instruction. There are other organized groups, such as the Iona Community in Scotland and Kirkridge in America, which combine a personal discipline of prayer and the devotional life with other forms of Christian action. More will be said of these in a later chapter, Yet these at best reach but a few. What is needed is a "grass roots" concern extending to the many.

In his *Alternative to Futility* published in 1948 Dr. Trueblood coined the phrase "the fellowship of the concerned," and the phrase has stuck as a designation for small groups, primarily of lay men and women, who take seriously the total mission of the Church with the devotional life as its contributory focus. For suggestions as to how such groups can be brought together in a local church or community, with their possible fruits and possible perils, the reader is referred to the symposium *Spiritual Renewal Through Personal Groups* edited by John L. Casteel. Such groups must have continuity for their full effectiveness, but the movement for an occasional week-end spiritual retreat also holds much promise. The title of a very useful book on this subject by Douglas V. Steere, *Time to Spare,* is suggestive both of a deep need of our time and of a continuing problem. It is taken from a sentence in the *Imitation of Christ,* "Blessed are those who are glad to have time to spare for God." [6]

So far, we have looked mainly at those functions of the Church usually centered in the clergy—the conduct of public worship, the administering of the sacraments, the giving of pastoral care to individuals through personal counsel and support. We noted the importance of the layman's response with certain appropriate obligations in the first two, and have observed the need and the possibility of his active participation as well as response in the ministry to the inner life.

Such thoughtful dedicated response by laymen ought never to be underestimated. Were such response by laymen vital in every congregation, the churches would have a vitality far exceeding what they now have. It could then be said of today's Christians as of those in the Book of Acts, "These men who have turned the world upside down have come here also" (17:6).

4. THE MINISTRY OF EVANGELISM

We look now at a form of service which in one sense comprises the total function of the Church as the carrier of the gospel of Christ, yet which has a specific focus. Evangelism is a term which can be used broadly as the lifting up of the Lordship of Christ over the whole of life, thus including everything dealt with in this chapter. It can be used also in the more restricted, yet vital, meaning of winning others to personal decision to enter upon the Christian life, and in a derivative though not identical sense, to accept membership in a Christian Church.

Evangelism ought to be present in every aspect of the life

[6] Trueblood (New York: Harper & Brothers); Casteel (New York: Association Press, 1957); Steere (New York: Harper and Brothers, 1949).

of a church. Whether in the Christian home, in the church school, in the fellowship activities of the church, in the ministry of counseling, in the Sunday morning worship service, or in special services directly labeled evangelistic, Christ ought to be exalted, His message to the whole of life indicated, a call to Christian discipleship presented. There are many ways to do this, and there is no requirement that a direct solicitation be made on occasions when other forms of Christian witness seem more appropriate and probably more effective. Yet this goal ought never to be lost sight of.

Here, as elsewhere, the minister has a great responsibility. Every sermon, whether or not it is specifically followed by an "altar call," ought to be an invitation to Christian discipleship. We ought to expect conversions to take place, and doubtless more would occur if more were expected. Though there is a place for mass evangelism through the voice and appeal of a Christian evangelist who views this as his particular calling, provided it is done with integrity and without hysteria, the most potent evangelism is that which takes place daily, weekly, yearly through the work of the local church.

But *does* it take place? That numerous good influences are extended through the churches can hardly be doubted. Yet such good influences very often fall short of evangelism. I have not seen this more pointedly put than by one who by profession is not an evangelist but a theologian:

> The pathetic exclusive preoccupation of some conservatives with gaining initial decisions for Christ rightly stirs an eager counter-concern to gain continuing growth in the Christian life. Unfortunately, much effort is made to cultivate Christian living in persons who have not committed themselves to Christ at all. . . . In the lives of such persons the basic evangelistic work remains to be done. No amount of good ideas or good works will avail for them until they have made the essential commitment of themselves to Christ.

This is not a matter of more gradual development. It is a matter of confrontation, of divine-human encounter, and of decision.[7]

Apparently what is being protested here is not gradual growth—every serious Christian, whether theologian or not, believes in Christian nurture—but the assumption that exposure to good ideas and good works will after awhile painlessly if not automatically make one a Christian. This assumption, though not often so clearly stated, is far too common in our churches.

What of the place of the layman in evangelism?

The first step, and to be realistic, for many it is a long step, is to make the personal commitment called for in the foregoing passage. Whether in some critical, life-shaking decision or in many smaller but equally serious decisions no less critical because less dramatic, one must decide to commit himself to Christ and resolve henceforth to endeavor to live in loyalty to Christ. Without this decision he is not yet ready to witness to others.

From this point forth, the evangelistic opportunity and responsibility of the layman appears in various forms. The most unstructured, but probably the most persuasive, is the fact that a devoted Christian witnesses by his total life in words, acts, and attitudes in a multitude of ways. To live among his associates the life of loving, resolute, and ever-consistent Christian integrity is of enormous importance. In some circumstances one may feel it appropriate to talk specifically about his Christian faith, in short, as it has been graphically put, to "gossip the gospel." [8] At other times the matter seems too personal. Nor is the layman wholly to be blamed for reticence at this point, for to ask the question "Are you saved?" or even

[7] From *The Case of Theology in Liberal Perspective* by Harold DeWolf. Copyright 1959 by W. L. Jenkins. The Westminster Press. Used by permission. P. 177.

[8] Cf. Hans-Ruedi Weber, "The Ecumenical Movement, the Laity, and the Third Assembly," *The Ecumenical* Review, XIII, No. 2 (January, 1961), 212.

the more modest "Won't you become a Christian?" is as apt to cut off communication as to induce conversion.

There are numerous new forms of evangelism, though not always so labeled, to be looked at in later chapters as signs of advance in the churches are examined. It may be noted here that the familiar "visitation evangelism" by which laymen go in teams to call on their unchurched neighbors has great potentialities if it is focused right and understood for what it is. Even with the best of training and good intentions, relatively few laymen feel that they can directly ask either their friends or strangers to become Christians. What they can do, both more freely and with hope of long range results, is to ask others to attend church with them and to affiliate with the church. Then within the orbit of Christian fellowship, if it is warm and genuine on the part of both minister and laity, Christian experience can mature and ripen.

In today's world Christian conversion and commitment most frequently come about through Christian nurture in home, church-school, and church activities, not through an abrupt, Damascus-Road transformation. That the latter can happen and has happened to empty, misdirected, or guilt-ridden lives in our time, no one can doubt. It is not the normal pattern, however, and we need not lament that it is not. Provided the impulse to the Christian life is strong, pure, and steady, with the words and acts and attitudes of other Christians speaking to one's inward need, God can work the miracle of transformed personality in any willing individual. This is conversion, however undramatic. There must be preparation for it, and beyond the initial decision there must be years of costing spiritual growth. To bring about such preparation, transformation, and growth is a primary function of the Church, and in it both minister and laymen are called to be God's humble, willing, and infectious instruments.

Evangelism is intimately connected with what has ordinarily

been termed missions, though "mission" in the broader sense of service to all mankind is a better term. As evangelism extends to the whole of life, so is the outreach of the gospel designed for the whole world. Though we must for convenience's sake still have boards and divisions of national and world missions, it is increasingly evident that the two are one. In the interrelatedness of our day there is no longer a "home base" and a "foreign field," no longer "sending" and "receiving" churches except in a financial and administrative sense. Even in administrative matters, there is increasing mutuality as the nationals of each country are appointed to posts of leadership while the missionaries become their assistants and fraternal workers. In the countries of the Orient there is a new outthrust of missionary endeavor from these to other lands. In the prevalent secularism of our time the United States is as truly a mission field as any, though there is need still for missionaries to be sent to both ancient and primitive non-Christian cultures.

What is significant about this for our study is that in the area of missions, distinctions between clergy and laity become less and less important. There are, to be sure, ordained ministers among those who go as missionaries from one land to another. Yet there are more laymen, and clergy and laity alike unite in a common task with many forms of service—educational, medical, vocational, and the like—in which clerical orders recede in importance before a common need. Albert Schweitzer is the Reverend Albert Schweitzer if one chooses to call him that, but who ever thinks of doing so?

If we do not here give more space to the missionary function of the Church, it is not from its lack of importance. Indeed, the very existence of the Church and the bringing of the gospel from Jerusalem and Judea to wherever we now live is the result of an impulse both evangelistic and missionary. All that has previously been said about evangelism applies to missions, regardless of geography. It is the business of the Church to serve human need wherever it exists, to speak of Christ wherever it is appropriate, to build up personality in every aspect, and by such service and active demonstration of Christian love to win others to Christ.

One point only in this connection needs to be emphasized. This is the obligation to reach out beyond the immediate to the need of "the uttermost part of the earth." Any church that spends most of its time, attention, or money on itself to the exclusion of concern for world need is bound to be not only parochial but enfeebled. Those churches have again and again proved strongest which gave most to others. The whimsical term "edifice complex" has come into vogue as a description of churches so involved in their own building campaigns that they cannot look beyond their own "lovely" sanctuary or new Christian education plant. Without attempting to disparage these activities, we must note that there seems often to be a distorted sense of what is important. Christ came to give Himself that all men might have the abundant life, and those churches are most Christian which follow Him in this mission.

5. THE MINISTRY OF EDUCATION

Side by side and interwoven with evangelism must go education. We noted above that for every decision for Christ there is a "before" and "after," a preparation and a follow-on in terms of progressive spiritual growth. All of this requires Christian nurture, a long-range educative process, and in short, a ministry of education.

If the reader has gone with me thus far, it need hardly be necessary to say that the ministry of education is not limited to the professional work of a trained person employed and designated as "director" or "minister" of Christian education. An honorable and serviceable profession this is, whether followed by clergyman or layman, a man or a woman. There ought to be more such persons of both sexes receiving such training and invited by churches to render their services. Yet our main concern at this point is with the work of the minister and the laity in the total service rendered to and by a church.

It is a major function of a church to appropriate, understand, and transmit its Christian heritage, applying the eternal truths of the gospel and the funded wisdom of the past to the contemporary needs of persons. The major source of this Christian heritage is the Bible, and with the denial of access to it in the public schools, we have a woefully illiterate culture in this respect. If knowledge of the Bible and its treasures of both literary and spiritual wisdom is not gained in the Christian home or church it will seldom be gained at all, except by the relatively small number who take a course in college and thereby find its treasure house unlocked.

Biblical *knowledge* is not enough. Its spiritual and ethical insights must be made applicable to personal, moral decisions and to the problems of living together in a world in which firm foundations have been largely broken up and much that seemed steady in the past is now in flux. To impart such Christian wisdom without dogmatism and to "lead out"—for that is what education means—the minds of children, youth, or adults is not an easy task, but it is an enormously important one.

There are four main channels for such education: the Christian home, the church school, the pulpit, and the adult forum or discussion group. Much excellent material has been written by others on the first two, and I shall not try to duplicate it. It need only be remarked that here is a channel for lay service of great potency and value. To bring up children not only in a Christian atmosphere, but also with steady encouragement to their church-school attendance and study and with patience in answering their inevitably theological questions is no small contribution to the ministry of education. To teach a church-school class with fidelity and adequate preparation, surrendering the leisure one might like to have on Sunday morning, is to have a part in an enterprise of incalculable worth.

Less general recognition is given to the fact that the pulpit too is a place for education, not for didactic homilies but for vital interpretation of the biblical message and the Christian faith. The pendulum in homiletics has swung between "expository"—or "exegetical"—and "life-situation" preaching. There is no need to choose between them if the proclamation of the gospel is the keynote, for a sermon can be, and should be, at the same time biblical, theological, and life-centered. There is no disparity between a brief explanation of the biblical setting, a clear affirmation of some important truth of our Christian faith, and its application to the needs of our times. Were this combination brought together more often there would be less need to introduce wisecracks and rhetorical flourishes to try to hold the listener's attention.

Yet the place par excellence for education is in a group where individuals can raise questions and talk back. In every organized activity of a church, whether in an adult church-school class, men's club, woman's society, or church family night, there is a place for instruction in our biblical and theological heritage and its application to contemporary life. The tragedy of it is that often such programs are devoted to entertaining trivialities or to themes that are good in themselves but have no basic Christian rootage—such as sports, flower arrangement, or the fauna of South Africa.

Again we find that clergy and laity must share responsibility. Ministers sometimes underestimate the desire or distrust the ability of their laymen to respond to significant educational content. Laymen sometimes fail to give their ministers sufficient encouragement by asking for it or by welcoming it eagerly when it is given. Yet the fact that again and again groups have "come alive" when they found that their basic questions were theological, with deep insights to be gleaned from our biblical heritage of faith, is sufficient ground for bolder ventures in this field.

6. THE MINISTRY IN AND TO SOCIETY

I shall say little about the social gospel, social service, or social action in this chapter because much of the remainder of the book will deal with it and with the layman's part in the ministry in and to society. It is enough to say in closing this chapter that the individual and social gospel, or better the individual and social ministry of service to which we are called by Christ, is an indissoluble unity. Variations in emphasis according to the occasion and to the theme under discussion there must be, but no splitting apart in substance. When the advocates of either one depreciate or try to exclude the other, not only is the gospel warped, but the aspect being advocated is weakened in its foundations and often distorted into a secularistic substitute for real Christianity. Whether what is being attempted is a psychological attempt to secure inner peace without paying the cost of a deeper devotion or a dramatic and even courageous attempt to secure social reform without a religious center, the temptation to substitute a humanistic set of values for the service of God besets the path of him who splits the gospel into sections.

Our reason for devoting more space in what follows to this function of the Church than to those already looked at is simple. It is not that it is more important, though it is not less so. Rather, it is here that the layman most directly witnesses and serves. If we grant that the clergy has the prior responsibility in the preaching of the Word and the administering of the sacraments, it is equally true that the laity has the prior responsibility within the world of home, school, community relations, politics, and a vast range of economic matters. The decisions by which society is regulated are almost wholly lay decisions. If Christian laymen do not assert themselves and live their faith in these areas which so intimately touch the lives of many millions, what is done in church will not matter greatly in this world, for there will be no world left to talk about.

Laymen have a great opportunity and responsibility for making society Christian. Yet the negative side of this relationship is equally present. Since the layman lives mainly within the world he is continually tempted to bring the standards, motivations, and procedures of the world within the Church. Not every layman yields to this temptation, and by no means is all the secularism of the churches due to lay influence. Yet secularism is there in formidable measure. Let us take a look at the various faces it assumes with some further inquiry as to whence it comes.

Chapter V

THE WORLD WITHIN THE CHURCHES

IN THE PREVIOUS CHAPTER WE HAVE LOOKED AT THE REGULAR, ongoing functions of a church—functions which are distinctive and give the Church a reason for existence not shared by any other community institution.

There are many tangent elements of service in which a church needs to do things that are also being done by other social agencies. Among these are such matters as vocational guidance, premarital counseling, and the holding of families together; the provision of wholesome recreation; the prevention of juvenile delinquency; the providing of happy fellowship and if necessary resident care for the elderly; the rehabilitation of alcoholics; the prevention or the reconciliation of industrial strife; the alleviation of poverty, ignorance, and disease; the challenging of racial injustice; the support of the United Nations; and the laying of foundations for world peace in an informed and active citizenship. As far as possible, what the Church does in these fields should be done in co-operation with other legitimate channels of public service, not in competition or in needless duplication of effort. The Church is not the only agency which God has ordained for doing good in the world.

Yet whatever the Church does, either within the world or within its own life, ought to be done from Christian motives and by Christian means. In some matters it is simply technical skills which determine effectiveness. and in these the churches ought not to be inferior to other agencies. In others moral issues are involved. The Church cannot engage in morally questionable practices and preserve either its own integrity or the strength of its witness. Some compromise in the rapidity of advance toward goals is inevitable, for goals are not arrived at in a day and perfection is seldom attainable. But compromise of basic intent and of Christian integrity must not occur. The Christian gospel provides no inflexible code for concrete decisions; yet it gives a directive in terms of the love of God and neighbor for every human situation. The word of Paul is still relevant, "Do not be conformed to this world but be transformed by the renewal of your mind, that you may prove what is the will of God, what is good and acceptable and perfect." (Rom: 12:2.)

In too great measure such conforming has taken place. This has weakened the witness of the churches, for when a church tries to conduct its affairs or speak its mind simply as one more good institution among many it might as well let the other institutions do the acting and speaking. To such lengths has this conforming been carried that we hear much about this being a "post-Christian" era and the substitution of "churchianity" for Christianity. As stated earlier, I believe these charges are often overdone; yet there is enough truth in them to provide a sobering challenge.

Since the primary purpose of this book is to help the layman to understand his church in its manifold aspects and hence his own place within it, we shall in this chapter note some ways in which "the world"—that is, our secular society—has so impinged upon the churches that the functions presented in the previous chapter have gone unfulfilled. Since the lay person in economic and political life comes usually into more direct contact with the world than does the minister, it is perhaps not too harsh a judgment to say that much, though not all, of this impingement comes from the layman's side. Yet the corresponding word to be said is that *because* of this direct connection, the layman's opportunity to make of his church what it ought to be becomes the greater. In any case, clergy and laity together must share the responsibility and assume the obligation.

1. WHAT IS SECULARISM?

In an earlier book, *The Modern Rival of Christian Faith,*[1] I have defined secularism as "the organization of life as if God did not exist." It is not an avowed atheism; it is not, at least in America, a direct attack upon religion. Indeed, where religion is popular, as it has increasingly become in America in recent years, secularism often solidifies its strength by favorable reference to religion, as in biblical quotations interspersed in political addresses. The word secularism comes from the Latin *saecula,* meaning an age or period, and secularism means conformity to the prevailing spirit of the age. Its impact is what the Bible refers to as that of "the world."

Secularism is not per se a derogatory term. A secular occupation is one that is not professionally religious, and most laymen are in such occupations. A secular state is one that has no particular religious affiliation and seeks to treat impartially all religious groups, and this is what the United States aims to do. It is when the secular gets out of bounds and usurps the prerogatives of the religious that it becomes a rival to Christian faith.

There is much about the spirit of our age that is good—for example, the prevalent interest in increased educational facilities, better health, comfortable and attractive living conditions, a humanitarian concern for the relief of suffering, an aroused sense of justice in regard to civil rights. Where such matters are advocated on a nonsectarian, civic, or social basis they ought not to be decried for being secular. Christians should rejoice that not only their fellow Christians, but others also are thus concerned.

As a fair sampling of what is covered by the term secularism,

[1] Nashville: Abingdon Press, 1952.

note the topics dealt with in a contemporary news magazine. In the index of a weekly issue of *Time* I find besides the "Cover Story," which may deal with a notable person in any field, the following topics alphabetically arranged: Art, Books, Business, Cinema, Education, Foreign News, Hemisphere, Letters, Medicine, Milestones, Music, National Affairs, People, Press, Religion, Science, Sport, Time Listings (of currently popular cinema, television, theater, and books). Of these only "Religion" bears any direct relation to the Church or to the Christian faith. Presumably these are the fields in which the general public is most interested. Other more specialized magazines may deal further with sex and love, family problems, cooking recipes, modes of reducing, styles, gardening, fishing and hunting, travel, market reports, popular science, and a multitude of do-it-yourself projects. While few persons if any have a consuming interest in all these fields, every person including every Christian had better be interested in some of them. To fail to do so is to retreat to the cloister and let the world go by.

If an interest in these areas is good, and if there are good things in all of them, why fuss about the presence of secularism in our churches?

The answer is so evident that it hardly needs to be made. The Christian gospel, being relevant to the whole of life, is related to all of these interests and many more. Yet it is not identical with any of them. The gospel proceeds from a distinctive center. The Church has a distinctive function, the central aspects of which were outlined in the previous chapter. The main business of the Christian, one who is "called out" though remaining in the world, is to exalt the Lordship of Christ over every interest. It is precisely because secularism sets up a wealth of interests from which Christ is usually left out that it becomes the modern rival of Christian faith.

What, then are the primary forms in which secularism invades our churches?

2. RELIGION IN GENERAL

The phrase "religion in general" is taken from a brilliant and penetrating exposition of the current plight of religion in America, Martin E. Marty's *The New Shape of American Religion.*[2] In what follows no summary or paraphrasing of Marty's thesis will be attempted and at some points, for instance the designation of this as a "post-Protestant" era, I differ with his judgment. Yet the book is extremely valuable for an understanding of the incursions of secularism upon our churches, and the term "religion in general" is an apt designation.

By religion in general is meant a rather diffused moralism, deferential to religion and often identified with Christianity, but without a distinctive center of loyalty or demand. It is an amorphous condition in which religion is prized as a part of our culture, even heralded in the recent so-called religious revival in America, but does not go deep enough to make much difference in either individual or social living. So amorphous is it that it defies exact definition, but it is most recognizable as good citizenship, tolerance of all faiths, and concern for the preservation of moral standards.

As good citizenship, it prizes democracy and "the American way of life." [3] In this attitude there is a blend of nationalism, practical humanitarianism, and the fruits of a Judeo-Christian culture. Aside from the ritualistic acts of public worship associated with the churches, the average American tends to think of religion as decency, fair play, kindliness, and observance of the Golden Rule. To the extent that he thinks about the meaning of democracy he rejoices that this is a free land "with liberty and justice for all," and he has at least a vague awareness that this freedom has religious roots. The linkage of Christian-

[2] New York: Harper & Brothers, 1959.

[3] Will Herberg in *Protestant, Catholic, Jew* (Garden City, N. Y.: Doubleday & Company, Inc., 1955), designates our common faith as the American Way of Life.

ity with democracy becomes especially pertinent when his country is threatened by an atheistic enemy.

It is no accident that appeals to religion have become good political propaganda. Not only are the sessions of Congress, in deference to long tradition, opened with prayer, but also national political conventions have invocations and benedictions, carefully allocated to stress our religious pluralism. Political aspirants quote the Bible, and eloquent references are made in political addresses to the religious faith of our founding fathers. Why? Motives are doubtless mixed. To curry favor with a public that still respects even when it does not perpetuate its religious heritage? A sincere expression of the importance of religion to moral stability? Who is to say?

It is not in political matters only that concern for freedom and decency blends with Christianity. It is found in the easy tolerance of all faiths that is in reality indifference and is signified by such clichés as "We all worship the same God," "We're all traveling the same road," or—worst travesty of all—"It doesn't matter what you believe so long as you live up to it."

This prevalent mood is discernible in an easy shift from one denomination to another according to geographical convenience and social congeniality as our rootless society moves from place to place. There is a place for the community church, and the movement toward church unity is not well served by too great rigidity in either theological beliefs or traditional churchly mores. Neither is it aided, however, or the kingdom of God advanced, by indifference to what a church believes in and stands for.

In the present great mobility of population, with one family in five on the move each year, several things may happen as a family moves to a new location. Attending the church of his denomination the first Sunday, called upon by the pastor and hopefully also by some lay members, the newcomer decides to affiliate and transfer membership. He and his family thereafter becomes active members of the church school and congregation. This is what ought to happen, but too often it does not. Sometimes he takes this opportunity to "shop around," attending a variety of services Sunday after Sunday. This may turn out well if he has the stamina to decide thoughtfully not only which church will best serve him, but which church he can best serve. Often it leads to never settling on any. Or he may decide to send the children to the nearest Sunday school and pick them up afterward. Or he may join the nearest church on the assumption that one church is as good as another. Or the family may simply sever its church connections.

In all of these possibilities except the first and a few notable exceptions in the second, it is not Christian commitment but religion in general that figures in one's thoughts and practice. Probably not many would go to the lengths recorded of two Baptists who moved to another part of the city, as the incident is told by John E. Skoglund.

> When asked about their present church relationship one of them replied, "The Baptist pastor used to tell us that if we move and cannot get to our church we should join a church in our new neighbourhood."
>
> The caller asked, "And what church did you join?"
>
> "St. Aloysius Roman Catholic," the woman replied. "And we can't tell the difference!"

Dr. Skoglund adds the comment, "While this person's ecclesiological perception must have been somewhat dulled, she presents in the extreme what is characteristic of so much of American Christianity, and especially Protestant Christianity." [4] Particularly is this true of mushrooming suburban communities where mobility is high, religion for the most part has

[4] "The American Free Church Tradition in the Movement for Christian Unity," *The Ecumenical Review,* XII, No. 3 (April, 1960), 319.

social standing, and denominational lines—far more than economic or racial lines—are blurred to indistinctness.

A further example of religion in general is the tendency to substitute "moral and spiritual values" for Christian faith and commitment. This is most explicit in reference to the public schools. There this emphasis must be viewed with sympathy, so long as the distinctions are not blurred, until some way is found to introduce into the schools nonsectarian instruction in our Judeo-Christian cultural heritage. It is not limited to the public schools, however, or even to character building agencies like the Boy Scouts and 4-H Clubs. Many a family where God is never mentioned, save in occasional expressions of profanity, and where church attendance is sporadically limited to Christmas and Easter, weddings, and funerals, nevertheless thinks of itself as Christian because there is some practice and inculcation of the ideals of a Christian culture. This is not to suggest that for a family to be Christian artificial standards must be set up and religious talk continually engaged in. Yet more is needed than a generalized desire to be good neighbors and to bring up the children to be decent citizens.

3. THE CHURCH AS A SOCIAL CLUB

Repeatedly in earlier chapters it has been noted that when a church loses its distinctive mission it tends to become a social club. It is time now to say more explicitly what this means.

What are the marks of a social club? Admittedly, there are many kinds of clubs, ranging all the way from learned societies to "pack rat" gangs. Nothing that can be said will exactly fit all of them. Yet in the clubs to which vast numbers of adults belong, whether the so-called service clubs like Rotary and Kiwanis, the fraternal orders, women's clubs, garden clubs, or bridge clubs, there are great similarities. As these similarities are outlined, it will become evident that there are great similarities between these and many a local congregation.

In the first place, a club consists of congenial, like-minded people. Despite occasional flurries as to office holding and control, a club consists of people who think enough alike to enjoy each other's company. If there are differences of opinion on controversial subjects like politics and religion they are either kept discreetly silent about or they are not serious enough to disrupt the unity of the group.

A reason for this like-mindedness is that while a club is joined voluntarily, usually by invitation on the initiative of someone already in the group, the existing members pass on the fitness of such new members. Sometimes by the "black balling" of unwanted persons, often by the subtle but equally negative action of suggested disapproval, some who might like to join are effectively kept out.

In the majority of clubs here being considered, the members are "nice" people, genteel, cultured, refined, well dressed. They do not appear unwashed; they do not eat their peas with a knife; they do not use conspicuously bad English. Their talk may be tedious and tiresome; their singing banal; and in some groups, their jokes a bit off color. But they do not transgress the mores of their station in their community.

A club usually has a focus, and often a humanitarian focus beyond itself. The service clubs do render service, even though the motto "He profits most who serves best" may not state the highest motive for service. Many a crippled-children's center, project to help the blind, school for the underprivileged, or old people's home has received substantial help from these sources. Such services are certainly commendable.

The clubs usually offer programs of education and instruction. Sometimes they are for recreation only; more often there is a program committee that provides an address, pictures, a demonstration, or something that adds a bit—sometimes a good deal—to one's store of knowledge and acquaintance with the world.

Finally, every club gives social fellowship, warmth of companionship, and not infrequently spiritual support to its members. Alcoholics Anonymous is a case of the latter. Most of the fraternal orders offer sympathetic help in time of bereavement or other trouble, and where it is needed, financial aid. The burial service of a deceased member, however artificial it may seem to an outsider, usually has behind it depth of meaning for those whose lives have been joined in a special kind of fellowship. It is not unusual for such a service to seem more meaningful to those within the fellowship than do the rites of the Church.

It is evident that clubs have about them much that is good —so much that people often prefer them to the church. This is not written to rail against them. Rather, it is to suggest the subtle ways in which secularism creeps into a church to make it one more club among the many.

There is a sense in which a church ought to be a fellowship of like-minded people. A church is a *koinonia,* a fellowship; it is also an *ekklesia,* a body of those called out with a central loyalty to Christ. The difference between a church and a social club does not lie in the fact of fellowship, but in the principle and Person that are central to it. A church exists to bring together rich and poor, educated and uneducated, of both sexes and all ages and of every nation, race, and color in an inclusive fellowship of which Christ is the head.

A church again is like a club in that membership is voluntary though usually upon invitation and expressions of a proffered welcome. Yet "whosoever will may come." A church turns its back upon the example and teaching of its Master if any are rejected because of race, status, or other forms of social cleavage. The actual congregations of today are regrettably altogether too like social clubs in their subtle forms of exclusion—a fact more true of the average Protestant congregation than of the Roman Catholic, where social lines are kept subordinate to the corporate worship of God *via* the fixed obligation of attendance at Mass.

This is intimately related to the fact that American Protestant congregations, usually without intending to be exclusive and often without awareness that they are, tend to be the stratified, middle-class, well-dressed, well-mannered, and "well-heeled" members of a community. There is no special reason why in clothes or manners the appearance of a Sunday morning congregation should differ from that of these same people at their club. But when social prestige or financial contributions become a criterion of acceptability outweighing inner integrity and Christian devotion, something is radically wrong.

The analogy need not in detail be carried further. Most churches do good works, provide instruction of a sort that may or may not be related to the gospel, give friendship to those within the fold and consolation in time of trouble. How far-reaching or deep-going these services are depends on the Christian insight and devotion of both the clerical and lay members. If the clubs or lodges do it better and thus attract attention, energy, or money that ought to be channeled through the churches, it may be due to the stronger appeal of secular forms of fellowship. However, the answer is not to be found in increasing the secularism of the churches. Rather, it lies in a searching self-inventory on the part of the churchmen in reply to the ancient question: "And if you salute only your brethren, what more are you doing than others? Do not even the Gentiles do the same?"

It is in the suburban churches of the present that religion is having its greatest opportunity, with new church buildings burgeoning and the church-school plants overcrowded with children. It is here also, in the midst of green lawns and "gracious living," that the temptation to social clubism is greatest. I have not seen this more vividly put than in an article entitled "Euphoria in Suburbia" by Waldo Beach in an Easter issue of *Christianity and Crisis.* It gains its pungency in part from the contrast between Gethsemane and Suburbia, but relates to ecclesiology as well.

I believe . . . in the holy Catholic church. Yet the actual ecclesiology of the layman in the main-line Protestant churches is that his church is a "club" of fine Christian people whose fellowship he enjoys. Nestled down among the ranch-type houses, deep in the forest of TV aerials, the new suburban churches find their members all birds of about the same native, white, middle-class feather, terribly self-conscious of their own kind. Congeniality is the main criterion in deciding which church to join, and respectability the criterion of status within the ranks. How can holiness and universality be achieved in churches whose real divisions are residential, racial, and economic?

The rituals of the churches of suburbia celebrate social harmony and economic affluence. The greeting of neighbors, the taking of the collection, the handshaking at the door ("I enjoyed your sermon."), may in plain fact be more significant transactions for many than the prayers of intercession or the Lord's Supper. *Agape* is taken to mean the friendly harmony that must prevail in the circle, "the tie that binds our hearts in Christian love." In this "club" ecclesiology, the minister's role is to fulfill certain priestly functions in an acceptably congenial way. On occasion he may preach prophetic sermons on generalized matters of brotherhood and peace, even justice, but the moral "offense" of Christianity should never be made local, to disturb the euphoria of the group.[5]

4. THE CHURCH AS A BUSINESS ENTERPRISE

A church like every other social structure must have a financial underpinning. It employs a staff, ranging in size from the occasional services of a part-time minister to several ministers and a large body of lay personnel. It must raise money to pay their salaries and, let us hope, send some into world service;

[5] XVI, No. 5 (April 2, 1956), 33. Used by permission.

it must keep up its property; it must pay its bills and debts, even investing funds on those rare occasions when it has any surplus; it must keep honest and accurate accounts that need not be hidden from scrutiny.

It is not to charge the Church with worldliness that these things need to be done. They are simply the economic, instrumental side of a spiritual enterprise, as necessary to it as the body to the human spirit. Or so it is in the modern world. In New Testament times, with congregations meeting in homes and with no paid ministry, the situation was simpler, but we cannot wish ourselves back into a bygone day.

Nevertheless, secularism finds numerous points of entrance into a church from the fact that it is a business enterprise. The most glaring of these is when churches are not quite honest with their finances, curtailing the benevolences to meet local expenses, "robbing Peter to pay Paul"—something that Paul himself would never have stood for—and juggling the books a bit to make things look all right. Somewhat allied to this is the practice of paying the nonministerial personnel less than their skills would command elsewhere on the assumption that they ought to work for less for the love of the Lord, or of keeping them overtime for unpaid hours of labor on the same assumption.

How prevalent are these practices? I know of no statistical data, but they occur. They occur often enough so that the National Council of Churches in an excellent statement on "Christian Principles and Assumptions for Economic Life" has had this to say:

> The churches themselves own property, invest funds, and employ labor. Often their policies have been no better than those which the Church condemns in the secular world. Its divisions often reflect and seem to give a religious sanction to the social divisions that are

characteristic of society at large. In all these matters judgment should "begin at the house of God." [6]

A subtle and pervasive form of secularism is the application to the church of the standards of success prevalent in the world of business competition. To judge the status or usefulness of a minister by his salary, or to do the same for a church by the splendor and costliness of its sanctuary, are cases in point.

In a business enterprise reports must be made and records kept. So it is in churches. But must numbers be made the central concern that they so often are in churches? It is difficult to make a mimeographed report or a statistical summary of the work of the Holy Spirit. Low figures may be a mark of apathy in a church; large figures are seldom a clear evidence of vitality, consecration, or Christian sensitivity. A fine record of membership, attendance, giving, or new conversions may be an occasion of humble thanksgiving to God; it is never a fit subject for boasting.

One of the most offensive of the secularistic impacts in this field is the idea of "selling" the gospel to the people. Because in both church work and commerce the needs of the people must be discovered or aroused and then satisfied as efficiently as possible, the temptation to salesmanship is strong. With it goes often the cheapening of holy things, the presentation of the gospel as a panacea instead of the demands of the cross. A common by-product also is the competitive spirit among churches, with a bonus in the form of promotion in rank and a bigger salary to him who proves the better salesman.

5. THE CHURCH AS A POWER STRUCTURE

This survey of forms of secularism within the Church would not be complete without at least a brief reference to a major

[6] Adopted by the General Board of the National Council of the Churches of Christ in the U.S.A. September 15, 1954.

issue—the struggle for power. We shall pass over large segments of history, wherein Church and State have contended for supremacy. We are here looking mainly at local churches and their denominational structure.

Does anyone doubt the existence of ecclesiastical politics? If so, he need only to attend a meeting of a major religious legislative body and witness the maneuvering that goes on in regard to controversial issues. In the election of important officials there is often not a little wirepulling, perhaps less by the candidates than by their chief supporters. Then after the election authority—not always, but sometimes—becomes authoritarian. Dictatorship is always the temptation of him who wields large power.

It is not only in the higher echelons of church leadership that this is visible. It happens in local churches too, when those who have long held office acquire the conviction, usually unconsciously, that they are indispensable. Then any effort to broaden the base of leadership and give responsibility to others is taken as a personal affront, and one clings tenaciously to power under the guise of fidelity in service. There is no dimension of church life that is immune to this temptation, and as an observer sees this happening to good Christians he is likely to be reminded of Lord Acton's famous dictum, "Power tends to corrupt; absolute power corrupts absolutely." Fortunately in a church there is seldom absolute power.

The dictatorial exercise of power has numerous sources, in which a desire for personal prestige and a sense of the need of firm action in exercising the responsibilities of office are often too mixed to be easily sorted out. It is not infrequently the result of inner insecurity and the loneliness that tends to accompany power. The more a person feels inwardly alone and not quite certain of his status with those about him, the more he tends to bolster himself by dominating others. This far-reaching fact has become a psychological truism. Churches and the Christians in them, whether clerical or lay, are no exception.

What has anybody in the Church to be afraid of? Is it not a fellowship of good will? Yes, and a reluctant no. It is not a sinless, secure, and altogether blameless fellowship; it is made up of mortal men and women with human frailties.

A contemporary analyst, speaking of ministers, puts it bluntly, "The clergy are afraid of lay leadership, of youthful initiative, of able women." [7] These formidable forces may, indeed, tempt the minister to demonstrate his sovereignty! Or they may reduce his utterance to innocuous platitudes on the assumption that he must not jeopardize his leadership and disturb the peace of the church. More often, perhaps, he is afraid of hostile criticism if he "sticks his neck out," afraid of loss of ecclesiastical favor, afraid of endangering the financial or social status of his family. The reader of these words, if he is a minister, may fill in or redraw the picture as he wishes.

What is the layman afraid of? This brings us to the last, and perhaps the most pervasive and subtle, form of secularism to be noted in this survey.

6. SOCIAL CONSERVATISM

The same analyst quoted above, a little earlier in the paragraph, pays the clergy a tribute in these words. "There is no doubt but that the American Protestant clergy as a group have a far more adequate conception of the implications of the Gospel for the whole community than have the laity, and have produced a series of prophets of some stature." [8] This I believe to be true. But why have the laity lagged behind the clergy in their grasp of the implications of the gospel for the community, and thus so often stifled prophetic utterance that might disturb the *status quo?*

[7] James H. Nichols, "Secularism in the Church," *The Challenge of Our Culture,* ed. Clarence Tucker Craig (New York: Harper & Brothers, 1946), p. 192.

[8] *Ibid.*

One answer is to be found in the thesis of the whole book—that the laity have too long been regarded and have regarded themselves as second-class Christians, their function being to help the minister run the church instead of their *being* the Church within the world. This is the general answer to the question, but there is a more specific answer that centers in the matter now under discussion—the relation between the exercise of power and a sense of insecurity. Let us illustrate in three crucial fields.

It is in general the laymen rather than the clergy who keep white churches white, who oppose integration in the public schools, who do not want civil rights legislation to be passed in Congress or placed in party platforms. Though there may be clergy who abet them in it from conviction, far more keep silent from what they regard as prudence. Almost every minister knows that racial discrimination, whether in the church or society, is contrary to the Christian gospel. Far more would speak out on the issue if they did not fear their laymen.

The laymen too are afraid. On the surface, there is the ever-present fear of intermarriage. Beneath the surface, there is the fear of loss of economic or political power through the rise in status of a suppressed people. The whole situation is shot through with the fear of disturbance to the cultural mores fixed and hallowed by long tradition.

To turn to another area, economic conservatism is the prevalent mood of the laymen of American Protestantism. The free enterprise system, even if not quite identified with the kingdom of God, is held to be so basic to the American way of life as to have a kind of holy sanction. The advance of Communism, with its real evils and dangers of which any discerning Christian is aware, has provided the occasion for attacks on both Christian and humanitarian liberals, whether in the Church, educational institutions, or politics.

As a result, the laymen of most congregations will listen somewhat responsively to pleas to help the hungry and homeless of other lands and will not be offended by sufficiently generalized statements about the message of the Hebrew prophets. But such presentations in regard to economic justice "should never be made local, to disturb the euphoria of the group." The issues in this area being less clearly drawn than in the matter of race, the ministers are themselves less certain what they would like to preach if they dared. The point, however, is that they seldom dare—nor will they until the laymen launch out more courageously. Speaking of the economic conservatism prevalent in our churches, George F. Thomas puts this significant question, "May it not be, therefore, that many Christian laymen resent the 'interference' of the Church on economic issues, not because the Gospel has little to say about them, but because what it does say is so disturbing?" [9]

In a third major area, that of nationalism, we come back to the point suggested earlier—that to many minds, to be a good American citizen and to be a good Christian are not very different terms. Accordingly the security of the nation and loyalty to its interests and demands take precedence over everything else. To many laymen—perhaps to most—there is no clear sense of contrast between the sovereignty of the nation and the sovereignty of God. To serve the nation is to serve God; what the State demands God requires. This is likely to be challenged quickly enough regarding events in another nation, such as the German Lutherans' obedience to Hitler or the South African Dutch Reformed Christians' espousal of extreme forms of racial segregation and discrimination in the policy called *apartheid*. Yet when it is a matter of one's own nation or locality the situation looks different.

This identification of patriotism with Christianity crops out

[9] *Christian Ethics and Moral Philosophy* (New York: Charles Scribner's Sons, 1955), p. 307.

unconsciously wherever there is any criticism of the current reliance on enormous military expenditures as a basis of security or any advocacy of a less hostile attitude toward Russia. It comes to sharpest focus over the issue of Christian pacifism. Most of the denominations in official statements have recognized the right of conscientious objectors to refuse participation in war on religious grounds, and this is now public law. In the emotional attitudes of Christians in local congregations, however, this right is far less generally accepted. There both pacifist youth and pacifist clergy are apt to encounter suspicion and censure. This is usually less true of the clergy than of young men of military age, both because of the traditional exemption of the clergy from military service and an inchoate feeling that there is some incongruity between war and Christian leadership.

With our society perplexed as it is with problems to which there are no clear answers, it is to be expected that opinions will sincerely differ on this and many other matters. Such differing opinions can be held in mutual understanding and Christian love within the fellowship of Christ's followers. What is ominous is the degree to which answers are sought, not through the insights and directives of the Christian gospel, but in the emotional attitudes of an all-engulfing nationalism. Examples are to be seen in opposition to the international outreach of the United Nations, in the tendency to advocate higher and higher military expenditures without much concern for humanitarian service through foreign economic aid, in the stifling of a free pulpit and other forms of freedom of expression, in the blurring of truth through inflammatory propaganda.

It is not the business of the Church, or of any Christian in it, to claim to have all the answers. It is the business of the Church to hold every proposed line of action up to Christian scrutiny —to throw the searchlight of the gospel upon every issue which affects the lives and destinies of persons in God's world. Ministers can do some of this; laymen by their closeness to the issues can do more—and do it more effectively—if they will.

In the next chapter we shall take some samplings from current issues which ought to concern Christians and try to note some directions in which Christians can move as the Church carries its gospel into the world.

Chapter VI

THE CHURCH WITHIN THE WORLD

IN THE PRECEDING CHAPTER, A NUMBER OF SPHERES OF INFLUENCE were outlined whereby "the world" in the form of the standards and practices of our secular society has impinged upon the life and witness of the churches. This was not done for the purpose of painting a dismal picture, for there is much residual health in the churches in spite of these factors. Nor were these sorry facts presented to castigate laymen for their part in bringing this situation to pass, for responsibility must be spread over a broad base. The chapter had as its purpose the need to see clearly what is wrong with us if we are to move forward to set it right.

In this chapter we shall not attempt to cover the whole gamut of matters for which churches—and more especially the laymen in the churches—should have a concern and in which action is called for. A few examples at important points must suffice. These will be presented under the covering captions of stewardship and mission.

1. STEWARDSHIP

Stewardship has most commonly been thought of in our churches as the giving of money for the support of the Church and church-sponsored activities. In theory this is not all that it is thought to comprise. Yet in practice, the Commission on Stewardship is also the Commission on Finance, and their responsibility is to raise enough money to meet the budget and keep from ending the church year in the red.

This is a worthy and necessary service. Though our Lord ranked spiritual treasure above material goods, it can hardly be supposed that God approves sloppy business dealings in a church under the cover of piety, or desires His professional servants to be less than adequately paid. As to how much is adequate opinions differ, and there are dangers in extremes at both ends. Yet it is a real form of stewardship when in gratitude for God's gifts laymen share their wealth or their "widow's mite" to provide the financial underpinning by which the work of the Church can go forward.

Stewardship in this form is usually associated with an appeal for tithing. To raise any question about the desirability of this practice is to invite criticism and possibly to run the risk of easing the conscience of someone now giving less than a tenth who ought to be giving more. Nevertheless, the question needs to be raised from the standpoint of genuine stewardship. If God has abundantly blessed us with material resources why give as little as a tenth, as if all the rest belonged to ourselves? Or if "the pinch of poverty" is real and not simply assumed from a false standard of values, may not God require the meeting of the basic human needs of one's family even if less than a tenth is given?

To illustrate, it is not uncommon in America today for laymen and indeed for some ministers, whether bishops, church executives, or pastors of large churches, to have a salary of 15,000 dollars a year, often with a generous expense account besides. If such a person thinks he has done enough when he gives 1,500 dollars of his salary and retains the rest to spend as he or his family chooses, it may be doubted that he is giving a good account of his stewardship according to the Pauline principle of giving "as he may prosper" (I Cor. 16:2). Contrast this situation with that of a Christian scrub woman whose husband has left her and who ekes out a living for herself and her four children by cleaning floors at night in a public building for

1,500 dollars a year. Does God expect her to pay the rent and keep the children clothed, fed, and educated on 1,350 dollars? It has been done, and the tithe gladly paid. But that the same percentage should be expected of all is, I venture to say, poor economics and poor religion.

Certainly in America there are many Christians whose stewardship ought to be reckoned on the basis of giving far more than a tenth to the church and charitable causes, and to exalt tithing as a fixed principle is to retreat before a God-given obligation. That tithing is "biblical" in the sense of being enjoined in the Old Testament is true, but so is the remitting of debts and the leaving of the ground fallow every seventh year, the leaving of sheaves in the field to be gleaned by the poor, the bringing to the altar of the first fruits of the fields and flocks and a lamb without spot or blemish, and much else that was suitable stewardship for early Hebrew society but is not for ours.

Stewardship in the full sense is derived from the Christian doctrine of creation. It centers in the conviction that "the earth is the Lord's and the fulness thereof" (Ps. 24:1), that all we have, whether of material, mental, or spiritual treasure, is the gift of God, and that we hold these gifts in trust. God has delegated to us a high responsibility in that He has commissioned us to "have dominion" not only over the fish of the sea and the birds of the air (Gen. 1:28), but over great power plants, wide expanses of mechanized industry and agriculture, electronics, aeronautics, atomic energy, and much else in our time.

If this be true, stewardship is much more than a matter of giving to the church and to church-related or charitable causes, though this is legitimately an aspect of it. It covers the getting, the spending, and the saving as well as the giving of money; the Christian use of all our economic resources; the investment of time, talent, energy, and, in short, of life itself in the way most consistent with the will of God.

In this comprehensive sense there is a stewardship of leisure time as well as of daily work, of family and business as well as of church relations, of mind and hidden thought as well as of overt output which the world observes. To be a steward of God's gifts in the fullest sense is to be a Christian in the whole of life to the fullest possible degree.

Nevertheless, in spite of this comprehensiveness of scope, stewardship comes most sharply to focus in the Christian's daily work when this is viewed as divine vocation.

What does it mean to be a Christian in one's daily work? Sometimes the emphasis is on injecting the devotional life into business, industry, and politics. This is illustrated by the gathering of businessmen or Congressmen for prayer breakfasts; the providing of meditation chapels in large plants, sometimes with stated services conducted by an industrial chaplain, sometimes intended mainly for quiet meditation in the coffee-break period; the lending of the names of well-known business, professional, or political leaders to the support of evangelistic campaigns or to the "religion in American life" emphasis. All of these are good things to do if they are done with sincerity and Christian devotion and not to enhance profits or prestige.

A second and perhaps more common understanding of what it means to be a Christian in one's daily work is to act with moral integrity and with eagerness to serve the needs of men in whatever calling one pursues. Thus, the physician seeks to relieve pain and to prolong life; the teacher to elicit mental and personal growth in the pupils appropriate to their capacities and level of development; the social worker or counselor to promote the adjustment of the maladjusted; the housewife to make a good home for her family and rear her children with healthy bodies and strong characters. To be a Christian in the complex processes of making or selling products may be more difficult because of the sharp competition and temptations to short-cuts in modern life, but it is characterized by a sense of service in what is made or sold and by a thoroughgoing honesty in the process. Likewise, the honest lawyer who will not make false statements or defend a person known to be guilty, or the legislator who speaks and votes according to the dictates of an enlightened Christian conscience, may be said to be exercising an important form of stewardship within his daily work.

This view of Christian vocation has been attacked on the ground that other persons besides Christians try to act with integrity in their work and that since neither business nor politics can be conducted with an idealistic moral perfection, the Reformation doctrine of justification by faith with the promise of forgiveness for the penitent sinner had better be put at the center of Christian vocation in daily work. According to this view the proper criterion for adequacy in Christan vocation is to be found, not in ideals of service, but in performing adequately the duties and demands of one's profession, in which there may be deep-seated moral ambiguities, and trusting to the accepting love of God made known in Christ. This position has been stated by Edward LeRoy Long, Jr., the editor of an important series of books on "The Christian in his Vocation," written by representatives of various fields. He rejects also "job-related piety" on the score that while it appears outwardly to relate religion and daily life, it actually tends to deepen the divisions between the sacred and the secular.[1]

I believe this challenge to be partially true. Neither church attendance nor acts of piety are all that God requires of a Christian, and they become bogus rather than real Christianity if not projected beyond themselves to be integrated with the totality of life. No Christian lives without sin either in his personal life or in his vocation, and we all stand in need of penitence as well as prayer. Every Christian ought to do his work as well as he can do it. So far, the challenge strikes at vulnerable spots.

[1] Note his article, "Christian Vocation in Practice," *The Christian Century*, LXXVII, No. 41 (October 12, 1960), 1179-81.

Nevertheless, this view of Christian vocation comes dangerously close to making the demands of the job, rather than the demands of the gospel, paramount. Granting the centrality of justification by faith, forgiveness is still only one side of the gospel message.

Few would question that the encouragement and practice of both corporate worship and personal devotions, on the one hand, and of moral integrity and the outreach to service of human need, on the other, are basic elements of the clergyman's ministry. Are they not equally so of the layman's? Are they not inherent aspects of the gospel message? Remove them and basic foundations, not only of Christian stewardship, but also of the total Christian life are shaken.

It will be recalled that the ultimate goal of the Church and of its ministry, says the Niebuhr-Williams-Gustafson report, *The Purpose of the Church and Its Ministry,* is the increase among men of the love of God and neighbor.[2] If laymen are in fact the Church within the world, called to a total ministry in their manifold vocations, then this goal is as true of the lay as of the clerical ministry, and if it is true, neither personal piety nor moral idealism can be set aside as inconsequential elements in Christian vocation.

What, then, does Christian stewardship mean in daily work within the circumstances of one's calling? Stated broadly, it means so to conduct one's self as to manifest and seek to promote the love of God and neighbor. Conceived more explicitly it has numerous facets, none of which exhaust the meaning in the term but certain of which need carefully to be taken into account. Among these are: (1) Personal awareness of and serious concern for the way of life set forth by Jesus as the will of God, with the recognition of the need to try to apply this directive to the changed conditions of our day; (2) The endeavor through both corporate worship and personal prayer to seek

[2] *Supra,* p. 88.

the leading of the Holy Spirit and strength for the daily task; (3) The choice of a vocation, in so far as the choice is open, in which there will be opportunities either for the direct or the more distant and long-range service of humanity; (4) The adaptation of talent and training to opportunity, so that one will be able to do his work well within his chosen field; (5) The refusal, even at personal cost, to work at an occupation one conscientiously believes to be destructive of human good; (6) The performance of one's duties with integrity, fidelity, and as much skill as possible in the job one does, including the many in which opportunities for service must seem remote; (7) The conducting of one's self on the job, as at church and everywhere else, with decency and dignity, with friendly relations toward associates, and according to standards one believes to be Christian.

This is not a blueprint for action. Even if these principles are accepted as valid, every individual must apply them within his own varied circumstances. In the attempt mistakes will be made; penitence is called for and the assurance of God's forgiving mercy is ever open. Yet to the degree that an earnest, dedicated effort is made along some such lines as these, the love of God and neighbor is increased and stewardship within one's daily work becomes an actuality.

It may be noted that in this list of guideposts, nothing is said about witnessing to one's faith. Does this mean it is unimportant or irrelevant? By no means! It is all-important, but there is more than one way to do it. Witness may include at times conversation which is recognizably religious, even consciously directed toward winning others to Christ, but this needs to be at appropriate times and in appropriate contexts. The prime essential is to witness to the gospel with the totality of one's working and one's living.

It was noted earlier that Christian stewardship relates to the spending and saving as well as the acquiring and giving of money. What a nest of problems this opens up in our luxury-loving, status-seeking, installment-buying society! The limits of space forbid going into them here. The reader who is interested to know what I might say further on this and some related subjects is referred to the chapter on "The Ethics of Economic Life" in my *Christian Ethics.*[3] Likewise the chapter on "Christian Faith and the Day's Work" in *The Modern Rival of Christian Faith*[4] contains some observations on this theme which I have seen no particular reason to change since the book appeared some years ago.

We turn now to the second of the categories under which we shall look at some continuing next steps, that of *mission*. Here, as in the stewardship of possessions or of labor but in a still more many-sided context, we must hold before us the ultimate objective of the love of God and neighbor. This, indeed, is what our mission is—but what does it entail as we seek to be the Church within the world?

2. MISSION

The Central Committee of the World Council of Churches, meeting at St. Andrews, Scotland, in the summer of 1960, issued a statement which in a remarkable way connects the notes of stewardship and mission and relates both to the place of the laity in the Church. It merits quotation at some length, though the limits of space prevent citing it in full.

> The Department on the Laity has been drawn by its work to consider not merely what the Church ought to be doing, but what the Church is. We have come to see that the *whole* Church shares Christ's ministry in the world and that the effective exercise of this ministry must largely be by church members, when they are dispersed in the life of the world. As was said in Evanston, "The real

[3] Nashville: Abingdon Press, 1957.
[4] *Op. cit.*

battles of faith today are being fought in factories, shops, offices, and farms, in political parties and government agencies, in countless homes, in the press, radio and television, in the relationship of nations. Very often it is said that the Church should 'go into these spheres,' but the fact is that the Church is already in these spheres in the persons of its laity." There is nothing new in this conception —for our Lord said, "Ye are the salt of the earth . . ."—but it is a truth which has been obscured over many periods of the Church's life.

The salt fulfills its function only if, after having been assembled and cleansed, it is scattered again to be dissolved. Likewise the Church lives by a process of assembling and scattering. It is brought together from all peoples, occupations and groups for worship and for other recognisable "organised activities." It is scattered as its members, and predominantly its lay members, disperse themselves in the life of the world. As salt fulfills its function only when scattered and dissolved, so an indispensable part of the ministry of the Church is exercised when the Church is in its scattered phase. This process of withdrawal and return, of being assembled and being scattered, is not accidental but essential to the Church's life.[5]

The most obvious way in which for many years the Church has been "scattered" and its gospel taken to many lands in response to the Great Commission is through the missionary movement. We have long had missions, whether labeled home or foreign missions. It is mainly by this projection of the gospel outward from the Church to the world through witness and service that the Church has encircled the globe. Though extending from the first century to the twentieth, it is chiefly in the nineteenth and the first half of the twentieth centuries that the missionary enterprise has been most far-reaching. In language, not of hyperbole, but of sober historical judgment Kenneth Scott Latourette has said of the missionary movement of this period that it "sent out tens of thousands of missionaries. They were

[5] Used by permission of the World Council of Churches.

supported by the voluntary gifts of millions of Christians. Never has any other set of ideas, religious or secular, been propagated over so wide an area by so many professional agents maintained by the unconstrained donations of so many millions of individuals."[6] Though these words are intended mainly to characterize the expansion of Christianity to foreign lands, home missions too through social settlements, schools for the underprivileged and those of minority races, orphanages, hospitals, and church extension to unchurched areas have done a vast amount of good in areas of special need.

Such missions began primarily in the evangelistic impulse to win the unconverted to Christ, but have more and more taken on the imperative of taking the Christian evangel to the whole of life through education, medicine, social work, vocational training, and much else. The results, even of evangelism in the narrower sense, have been far-reaching and often unpredicted. In his enthronement address as Archbishop of Canterbury, the late William Temple made an oft-quoted and frequently misquoted statement. Speaking of the world-wide outreach of the missionary enterprise and its endeavor to proclaim the gospel for the winning of an eternal salvation, he said, emphasizing its humanly unplanned but God-given fruitage, "Almost incidentally the great world-fellowship has arisen; it is the great new fact of our era."[7] While these words do not, as is usually assumed, refer directly to the ecumenical movement, there is a basic appropriateness in linking together evangelism, missions, and ecumenicity. When the Church proclaims its gospel faithfully, men are drawn toward Christian unity.

Missions must go on, whether in foreign lands or in our midst, whether in the rising tide of nationalism through "fraternal workers" or in persons still called missionaries, whether

[6] *Anno Domini* (New York: Harper & Brothers, 1940), p. 169.
[7] *The Church Looks Forward* (New York: The Macmillan Company, 1944), p. 2.

in the legitimate breaking down of former distinctions between "sending" and "receiving" churches or by way of both denominational boards and ecumenical agencies, whether in conflict with resurgent indigenous faiths or an all-pervading secularism. Each of the phrases in the preceding sentence, with numerous others that could be added, suggests a large issue in current missionary procedure and strategy. It is not the purpose of this chapter to pursue these issues. The statements issued by mission boards, the reports of conferences, the missionary magazines, and the study books are full of these matters, which laymen as well as clergy ought to learn about and consider intelligently, sympathetically, and seriously.

Many more of our most talented Christian young people should be responding to the call for missionary service. Much more money and effort ought to be going into missionary channels, for the day of missions is by no means past. This cannot be said too clearly or emphasized too forcefully. Yet there is another, and a related, matter of equal urgency. This is the central importance, not of missions only, but of *mission.* Mission is many-sided, but not the least of its aspects is in the field of social action.

As an indication of the comprehensiveness of the Christian mission in this area, the Methodist Board of Christian Social Concerns has marked out thirty-five vital areas in which Christians of today, Methodists and others, should have a social concern. I list them to suggest the range of current social issues. These if analyzed according to special problems within each would include many more. The heading indicates the Board division to which responsibility in each of these various fields is assigned.

Division of Peace and World Order. American foreign policy; United Nations and related international organization; disarmament and nuclear weapon control; space control; foreign aid; tariffs and trade; immigration and naturalization; military policy and conscription legislation; conscientious objectors and the draft.

Division of Human Relations and Economic Affairs. Race relations; civil liberties; public policy on education; Church and State; population mobility; civic responsibility; urban redevelopment; labor-management relations; agriculture; conservation; government and private economic policy and practices; technological change; unemployment; housing.

Division of Temperance and General Welfare. Alcohol problems; addiction to injurious habits such as use of tobacco and drugs; gambling; pornography; juvenile delinquency; crime; penal system and rehabilitation; mental health and medical care; problems of the aging; population; planned parenthood; traffic safety.[8]

Can any layman look at this list and feel that his Christian obligation, in short, his mission is fulfilled when he pays his pledge, ushers on Sunday, attends the meeting of his church board? Important though these are, they are not all that is required of a Christian.

Readers whose memories reach back to the Oxford Conference on Life and Work in 1937 will recall the challenge expressed in the words, "Let the Church be the Church!" They were a rallying cry to fidelity to Christ in days that were soon to test to the utmost the fidelity of Christ's followers. We live in an equally serious and in some respects far more ominous situation in this nuclear-space age. To assume that the Christian Church should limit its message and ministry to "spiritual" matters, leaving aside such social concerns as those listed above, is to make of it a conventional and in some personal matters helpful institution, but it is to fail tragically in our mission to a world in grave need.

[8] The list is taken from *The Methodist Story,* Vol. 5, No. 6 (June, 1961), p. 30, though in the discussion which follows I have followed the order of an earlier listing.

If we are to fulfill our mission for the increase of God and neighbor in these fields, it is for the most part laymen who must act. Ministers and theologians can speak, write, stir, and sometimes clarify the issues; laymen live with these issues daily and must do most of what is done about them. Without presuming to do more than to point some directions, let us glance at a few of these areas for illustration. Because of its prime importance, the first item in each list will be selected. So, what of American foreign policy?

First, a word is in order as to whose responsibility these things are. The great decisions must be made by the President, by the Congress, by the State Department, and by technical experts and advisers who may happen to be Christian laymen but who are not selected for their competence in this relation. In short, there is a considerable degree of remoteness from the rank-and-file layman in the ordinary church. Because of this fact many laymen feel that it is "the government" that decides these things, and in spite of their right to vote they do not feel themselves a part of the government. While nobody wants a third world war and while political interest mounts toward election time, a feeling of remoteness from direct responsibility encourages ignorance and indifference to crucial matters of foreign policy.

Futhermore, so complex are these issues that there is no full agreement even among the wisest minds and the best of Christians. Conscientious differences of opinion can be found all up and down the line.

Confronted by this dilemma, is the layman who worships on Sunday morning in his church along tree-lined Main Street to be simply a casual onlooker at what happens in his nation's capital or at the U.N. headquarters along the East River? Is he simply angry or amused at Khrushchev's antics, and does he come away from watching television debates either confirmed in his prejudices or without opinions of his own? If so, he is not accepting his mission as a Christian.

It is every layman's duty (1) to be as fully informed as possible about international relations in today's world; (2) to take into account what ought to be done, not only for the security of his own nation, though this is important, but also for the demands of world order, the welfare of other nations, and service to their people; (3) to be open-eyed as to the evils of Communism, yet to recognize the need of living together in a divided world; (4) to vote these convictions and to let them be known as occasion arises; (5) if the issue comes to a clash between the will of the State and a higher loyalty, to "obey God rather than men."

Such a program calls for action. It is likely to mean, among other things, study groups, conferences, and seminars for the acquiring of knowledge and the interchange of ideas; the writing of letters and the sending of telegrams to one's representatives in Washington so that the weight of public opinion may be felt; and the dissemination of information and peace-mindedness through books, pamphlets, bulletin boards, movies, club programs and every available and appropriate channel, and most effective of all, by personal witness. It means, in short, the willingness to "stand up and be counted," even when to state a point of view is to stand against the tide of popular sentiment, for it is in the impact of life upon life that attitudes are most often molded. For some laymen, though not necessarily for all, it may mean taking the course of conscientious objection to participation in military service. Upon all laymen rests the obligation to respect Christian differences of opinion when these are conscientiously held and courageously adhered to.

To return to the list of topics cited under "Peace and World Order," in spite of the complexities inherent in these matters a considerable consensus has been reached within ecumenical bodies and in denominational pronouncements. There is no dearth of material on these points; there is so much, indeed, that its profusion is sometimes bewildering.[9] The concerned Christian citizen needs to keep abreast of current events in conjunction with such directives. At the risk of oversimplification, the general direction of the consensus reached by the responsible churchmen may be briefly stated in terms of a comment on each of the fields of concern enumerated in this list:

1. American foreign policy must be geared, not alone to the security of this country, but to the establishment of peace with justice in the international community. The preservation of democracy with moral strength and integrity at home is essential to its preservation on the world scene.

2. The United Nations merits moral, political, and financial support. It should not only be supported, but also should be strengthened and improved. In addition to its social services, it has prevented wars and continues to prevent them. Its General Assembly provides a sounding board for the moral sentiment of the world, and to bypass the U.N. for unilateral action is to imperil the peace of the world.

3. Progressive, multilateral curtailment of the arms race is essential to the peace and welfare of all nations. To protect present and future generations from the effects of radiation fallout, nuclear testing must be ended.

4. Outer space belongs to all mankind. Its penetration should be for scientific rather than military ends, with discoveries freely available to all.

5. Technical assistance to underdeveloped peoples on a hu-

[9] The Department of International Affairs of the National Council of Churches, 475 Riverside Drive, New York 27, N. Y.; the Peace and World Order Division of the Methodist Board of Social Concerns, 100 Maryland Ave., N.E., Washington 2, D.C.; and the Friends Committee on National Legislation, 245 Second St. N.E., Washington 2, D.C. are excellent sources of study materials. The reader is referred also to the headquarters of the social action agency of his own denomination and to the many articles, including many that are highly significant, in *The Christian Century* and the various denominational periodicals.

manitarian basis is a fundamental duty. Whether or not military aid accompanies it, economic aid should not be tied to military advantage.

6. World trade, with a considerable freedom in the flow of goods from nation to nation, is essential to the economic health and domestic stability of every nation, and hence indirectly to peace and world order.

7. While immigration and naturalization must take place under controls, the present restrictions on immigration are unjust and need revision. They are based on an out-dated quota system and give too little opportunity for the admission of refugees and others well qualified to be good citizens.

8. Though church pronouncements have varied as to the degree of support affirmed for military strength, it has been said repeatedly that military power alone is not enough. Most of the churches in the past, together with the National Council of Churches, have spoken against universal compulsory peacetime conscription. After two decades of it, the protest now appears to be less strong than formerly.

9. Christian pacifism has always been, and still is, a minority sentiment in all the American churches except the "historic peace churches." [10] Nevertheless, the right of conscientious objection on religious grounds is commonly granted in official statements.

Here we must leave these matters, and ask the reader to discuss, amplify, or reject these positions as he will. The two things I would urge him not to do are to suppose that Christian good will alone is enough to settle all these issues and to assume that as a Christian he has no responsibility in the matter. What each one of us as a Christian citizen thinks and does matters enormously, so much, indeed, that on our corporate Christian political witness may hinge the fate of the world.

[10] This term is commonly used to refer to the Society of Friends, the Mennonites, and the Church of the Brethren.

The Church Within the World

The limits of space make it necessary to restrict comment on the many fields in which laymen have a mission to be the Church within the world. We shall now take a brief look at the enormously important area covered by the first item in the second list.

The matter of race relations is a very personal and immediate issue; yet at the same time it is as world-related as anything in the sphere of peace and world order. If one were to try to state the gravest issues confronting mankind today he would certainly have to include, along with the possibility of a third world war and the menace of Communism, the injustices and tensions stemming from racial prejudice and discrimination.

The matter is directly related to everybody in the question of whether persons of a minority race—or, as in South Africa, of a majority but suppressed race—will find equal opportunities and a friendly welcome in church, school, business, and recreation; voting and office holding; medical and other social agencies; the use of public facilities including transportation, lunch counters, and rest-rooms; and the freedom to live in any area when they can afford to do so and will conduct themselves with decency and dignity. The issue is not primarily one of intermarriage, though this is indirectly related to it and that is the bogey that always raises its head whenever equality of fellowship in any of these other spheres is mentioned. Viewed from the standpoint of these other matters, which ought to be open to anybody in a free country "with liberty and justice for all," is there a community in America which is free of race discrimination? Though the degree of freedom varies widely, it is doubtful.

The problem is world-wide, again varying widely from place to place, but forming a miasma of injustice, dominance, and discontent which from time to time becomes overt but is always present as a subtle poison. This eats into the personality of the oppressor as well as oppressed, undermines social stability, and by the repudiation in practice of the democracy so readily professed, forms a fertile field for the seeds of tyranny to grow in.

There is no simple blueprint or single track to follow in combatting it. Yet here, perhaps more directly than in any other social concern, laymen have an immediate opportunity and responsibility. The place to begin is in searching one's own soul for latent seeds of prejudice, then one's own church and community. There is no other major social issue on which churches have spoken so unanimously and unequivocally as to what is right and Christian; there is none in which the churches themselves are so far at variance in practice with what is stated in affirming Christian principles. The place to begin is the closing of this gap.

This is the place to begin, but not to end, for legislation and the enforcement of legislation are essential, and laymen for the most part hold this in their hands. Community attitudes must be changed—some would say before the legislation, but the two must go along together lest each approach await the other and nothing be done. For example, school desegregation by Supreme Court decision and Federal Court order proceeds smoothly and without incident where the people are willing, yet these same people in many communities would not have desegregated their schools without a legal push in this direction.

Incidents are bound to occur when familiar social patterns of long standing are challenged. These incidents can be destructive when ill feeling runs high and violence breaks out, but they can also be constructive, educative, and a forward step—short or long—toward a Christian recognition of human dignity and a democratic equality of persons. There have been outstanding examples in recent years of nonviolent persistent demonstrations by Negroes to secure their rights in a free society, demonstrations undergirded by prayer and engaged in with calculated risk of danger but with a deep sense of Christian imperative. Some of these were led by clergymen, and the name of Dr. Martin Luther King, Jr. is likely to live in history for setting before the world what many had said was impossible—a clear example of the power of concerted Gandhian non-violence amid the complexities of American society. Yet the majority of the participants who walked instead of taking segregated buses, or who sat unserved at segregated lunch counters, or who defied transportation restrictions and went to jail were laymen. Other laymen in other parts of the country and not directly implicated in these particular movements may well be stirred by this example of persistent courage to support by voice, vote, and if necessary by nonviolent action, whatever is needed to secure racial justice in their own communities.

To move now into some discussion of the social problem which heads the third list, a different situation prevails from that in either of the first two. Everybody wants world peace, but there are marked differences as to the road to follow to arrive at this goal. Virtually all Christian pronouncements and the great majority of Christian individuals give pen and lip service to the idea of the equality of all persons before God, but in practice high racial barriers with accompanying rationalizations are set up. In the field of alcohol problems, however, alcohol*ism* is never condoned; yet wide latitude exists, not only among Christians, but among churches as to whether moderation or abstinence is the answer.

Let us begin by recognizing that a good many false, or at least unconstructive, attitudes are prevalent in the churches. On the one hand, there is a general distaste for hearing about the problem on the ground that "we don't drink and it's not a problem here," "the subject has been talked to death," "it's everybody's own business." Subconsciously, laymen may recognize that current business and social practices put them in an embarrassing spot if they do not drink, and they would rather not hear about it.

The "opposite number" is the setting up of the liquor problem as the paramount, if not the sole, social evil with total abstinence as the paramount virtue. This attitude, however sincerely held, is often tinged with a touch of self-righteousness and almost always carries with it a sense of shock that another Christian should think it legitimate to sip a cocktail.

Perhaps the most fruitful attitude is in neither of these directions. I am a total abstainer and honor the emphasis which my church (the Methodist) has long given to this position. The liquor problem is a very grave one, taking every year many lives through drunken driving, wrecking homes, causing economic loss, bringing about much deterioration of personality and great unhappiness. To be indifferent to it is to act the part of the proverbial ostrich.

On the other hand, we need to remember (1) that it is primarily a sickness of our current society, with many factors involved besides the sin or the weakness of the person who drinks; (2) that it needs to be attacked, not with sentimental indignation or self-righteous pride, but rationally, objectively, and with sympathetic understanding; (3) that there are sincere Christians, even deeply dedicated Christian leaders, who believe it is possible to drink in moderation without offense against God; (4) that laymen far more than ministers are subjected to temptation in this area; and (5) that laymen far more than ministers can help to solve this problem by the witness of personal abstinence, by words where words are appropriate, and by the enacting and enforcing of legal restraints.

Some further elaboration of the last two points may be in order. At a social function a minister, unless he is of a denomination that counsels moderation rather than abstinence, is seldom expected to take a cocktail. His hostess as a matter of course offers him tomato juice or a soft drink, and social expectancy protects him from embarrassment. Not so with the layman, unless he already has a rock-ribbed reputation at this point, and still less is it true of the young layman who feels that he must conform if he is to rise in his profession.

The answer is not conformity or withdrawal from society, but stability in conviction. Nondrinkers who find this easy because social expectancy is on their side had better recognize that for hosts of their contemporaries it is not easy. The answer does not lie in denunciation, but in an unremitting long-range effort so to change the patterns of society that the person who does not want to drink will have the support of his peers in his refusal. In this process laymen obviously hold the key.

Much has been said of the Prohibition era and its failures. That there were failures in enforcement, with bootlegging and speak-easies rampant, cannot be questioned. This is not to say, however, as is too often lightly said, that restraint by legislation is futile. As one whose memory goes back to the Prohibition era, my impression is that there is far more drinking now—at least more evidence of drinking, with more serious public consequences—and law-breaking certainly has not disappeared. In any case, the end of Prohibition was not the end of the problem! This is not to advocate a simple reversion to the former pattern, but it is to suggest that a combination of social education and legal restraint is imperative, and that in both fields laymen have a prime responsibility.

One is tempted to go on down the list to, in particular, juvenile delinquency; crime and the penal system, especially the moot subject of capital punishment; mental health; problems of the aging; the population explosion and planned parenthood which are much in the public mind today. There is a Christian approach to all of these matters in terms of that love of God and neighbor which calls forth respect for personality, with a sympathetic understanding of the human situation which precipitates these problems and of the persons who must take the brunt of them. The techniques for dealing with them are available; what is most needed now is a caring, personally costing, desire to use these procedures in the most helpful and constructive way.

In none of these fields can the Church alone solve these problems which are the common concern of a pluralistic society. In virtually all of them the churches have agencies which can be helpful. Yet transcending in importance the mechanics of these many channels of social amelioration is a spiritual factor—the concerned interest, personal activity, and moral support of Christian laymen. Such lay persons, whether professionally involved or simply citizens making their contribution through voice and vote, can tip the scales towards human dignity, freedom, and the more abundant life for all.

Chapter VII

SIGNS OF ADVANCE

IN THE TWO PREVIOUS CHAPTERS WE HAVE LOOKED AT THE IMpingement of the world upon the Church and, reciprocally, some of the channels through which the Church through its laymen could make a deeper and more effective impact on the world. Stewardship and mission were the keynotes in this approach. This is not simply an ethereal dream, for important beginnings have been made. Enough has already been done, with enough fruits, to point the way forward.

This chapter will be devoted to a descriptive statement of some of the most significant of these projects and movements. All have emerged within the past half century, and some quite recently. Those to be described have been in existence long enough to have proved their usefulness. There are others which the limits of space will require us to pass over.

These movements take a variety of forms and in general are independent of each other. Yet they have some common presuppositions, arising out of the situation and a sense of need rather than from any organizational structure. Let us begin by noting what these are.

1. COMMON FOUNDATIONS

First, these enterprises have a common center and point of reference. This center is God's yearning concern for the whole world and His supreme gift of Jesus Christ for the salvation and upbuilding of men. This concern includes all persons in all lands and cultures and—what is more commonly overlooked

—in all aspects of their lives. The most familiar verse in the Bible, John 3:16, could be taken as the charter of all of these movements, though in no narrow or other-worldly context. What is basic to them all is that as they reach out in many ways to the service of the world all are Christ-centered. All attempt to bring the message of the Incarnation into contemporary life. They rest on the assumption that good ideas and good works without personal Christian commitment can no longer, if ever, be viewed as adequate. In short, to use a convenient phrase that sums up much, all these movements have a vertical reference.

Yet all of them have a horizontal reference as well. All are protests against making individual purity or personal piety into a form of spiritual self-indulgence or a flight from the sordid and tragic needs of the world. This has been put graphically by George MacLeod, the founder and leader of the Iona Community:

> I simply argue that the Cross be raised again at the centre of the market-place as well as on the steeple of the church. I am recovering the claim that Jesus was not crucified in a cathedral between two candles, but on a cross between two thieves; on the town garbage-heap; at a crossroad so cosmopolitan that they had to write his title in Hebrew and in Latin and in Greek (or shall we say in English, in Bantu and in Afrikaans?); at the kind of place where cynics talk smut, and thieves curse, and soldiers gamble. Because that is where He died. And that is what He died about. And that is where churchmen should be and what churchmanship should be about.[1]

In the third place, all have a common center in accenting the importance of theological and biblical understanding. Some do this on a very advanced basis, as in the Faith and Order Commission of the World Council of Churches where many of the outstanding scholars of the Christian world are at work. Others,

[1] *Only One Way Left* (Glasgow: The Iona Community, 1956), p. 38. Used by permission.

as in the laymen's institutes, study the Bible and the Christian faith chiefly for the light that is thrown on the problems of daily work and living. But all take seriously the need to understand the Christian faith and to find a basis for this understanding in the Bible.

In the fourth place, all recognize the centrality of worship, not worship as a personal luxury inducing complacency before the need of the world, but worship so centered in God and the Cross of Christ that at the same time it stirs to social action and imparts inner courage, peace, and hope.

And, in the fifth place, all are adventures in fellowship. In some of these movements the organizational structure is elaborate and intricately interwoven, as in the National Council of Churches. In others—and this is the more common tendency—there is only enough organization to provide a body to function through. Yet all aim to make fellowship primary. Each recognizes the importance of the impact of life upon life in a fellowship of study, work, and worship, and the need to serve God and neighbor not in isolation but in community. In fact, "community" and "koinonia" have become current diction.

Finally, all recognize the importance of the laity both within the Church and as the Church within the world. It is because of this that these particular movements have been selected to be outlined here.

2. THE ECUMENICAL MOVEMENT

Reference has already been made to the ecumenical movement in the earlier chapters of the book. The chapters on how we got our denominations were intended to serve several purposes: to clarify further the nature of the Church, to show in historical perspective the place of laymen within it, and to assist in understanding the grounds both of the agreements and differences among the various families in the household of

Christian faith. We must now look at the relation of laymen to the main structures of ecumenicity.

Laymen are not so closely related to the ecumenical movement as they might be, and might well be. There is a hiatus between the "overhead" and the "grass roots" that is of serious proportions. Yet taken as a whole, the very existence of the ecumenical movement, whether it is in the World Council, National Council, or local manifestations, is a great step forward in Christian fellowship and co-operative action. The investigative, educational, and service programs launched, the united services of worship spanning denominational and other man-made lines, the conferences held, the statements adopted and commended to the churches for study reveal a high degree not only of Christian unity but of Christian wisdom and insight among those who have caught the vision of "one Lord, one faith, one baptism."

In this wisdom, in spite of differences sincerely held and usually mutually respected, there is far more agreement than division. The pronouncements made by ecumenical gatherings, though they often fail to scintillate in style because they represent composite thinking, are of genuine importance because they represent a high degree of consensus among informed and serious-minded leaders. This is not surprising, for these leaders tend to read the same theological books and interdenominational journals and to share a common point of view as to the need of evangelistic and missionary advance, racial equality, and the rightness of "a nonsegregated church in a nonsegregated society"; technical assistance to underprivileged peoples; support of the United Nations; service to refugees; a realistic grappling with the problems created by technology and rapid social change, and much else.

Such conferences thus far have not had nearly enough lay people as delegates, and both from the standpoint of what laymen have to contribute and of what they might receive to pass on to other laymen, the representation needs to be increased. This is particularly true of lay women, whose capacity for effective leadership in the denominational women's organizations has been clearly demonstrated. Delegates to ecumenical conferences are most often chosen from among the bishops, leading clergy, board secretaries, and other established denominational leaders. Relatively few representatives of industry, agriculture, the social agencies, teaching, medicine, statecraft, or homemaking are among them. This omission not only impoverishes the conferences but is a reason why ecumenicity does not go forward more rapidly at the grass roots.

Nevertheless, in both the World Council of Churches and in the National Council there are departments and activities dealing with matters of great importance to laymen. We shall glance rapidly at some of them.

The World Council of Churches was launched after the Oxford and Edinburgh Conferences of 1937 with the merging of the Life and Work (social issues) interests with the theological studies of Faith and Order. At the Amsterdam Assembly of 1948, when the World Council of Churches was fully constituted after having been "in process of formation" during the interim, there was a subcommission that studied "The Significance of the Laity." It was soon recognized that this was too important an issue to be thus subordinated, and the Evanston Assembly of 1954 had one of its six sections, with a full-scale discussion, devoted to the layman in his vocation.

This interest has continued. At Evanston a Division of Ecumenical Action and a Division of Studies were set up to direct the long-range work of the Council. Within the Division of Action there is a department on the laity, under whose direction studies in this field are continually being made, information gathered and disseminated, and interest promoted. Twice a year an informative bulletin is published. Any concerned layman would do well to subscribe at very modest cost to the bulletin, entitled simply *Laity,* which can be secured through contacting the American office of the World Council of Churches.[2]

Furthermore, since the laity is the Church within the world in its manifold aspects, other activities and interests of the World Council should be of much concern. Within the Division of Ecumenical Action there is also a Department of Co-operation among Men and Women in Church and Society. This department was broadened at the Evanston Assembly from its earlier title of "The Life and Work of Women in the Church" to cover this wider scope of co-operation, and has made important studies not only of the moot subject of the ordination of women (at the request of the Church of Sweden) but of the professional and volunteer service of women in many parts of the world. The relation of this field to lay interests is suggested by the fact that the author of the most useful book which has been written in this field, *The Service and Status of Women in the Churches,* is an English woman, Dr. Kathleen Bliss, who was chairman of the section on "The Laity—The Christian in His Vocation" at the Evanston Assembly.

The Division of Action has a youth department under whose direction numerous ecumenical work camps are conducted each summer, bringing together young people of different national, racial, and church backgrounds to engage in works of Christian service and to experience the rich variety within Christian fellowship. There is a Department of the Ecumenical Institute, with contacts reaching out to the many laymen's institutes of which we shall speak in the next section, but with special responsibility for the Ecumenical Institute at the Chateau de Bossey near the Geneva headquarters of the World

[2] The address is that of the new and beautiful Interchurch Center, which houses the headquarters of various denominations as well as those of the National and World Councils, 475 Riverside Drive, New York 27, N. Y. The subscription price of the bulletin (formerly called *Laymen's Work*) is one dollar a year.

Council. Here Christians of all races and of many nations, languages, and Christian communions meet to discuss together the challenge offered to the Church by the secular world and to engage in corporate study of the Bible in relation to the problems of one's daily work and vocation.

It must be apparent by now that the activities of the World Council which concern laymen are by no means limited to what goes on within the Department on the Laity. Among other activities, some of the most dramatic and far-reaching have been the services of the Division of Interchurch Aid and Service to Refugees, whereby well over 100,000 refugees have been helped to resettle in other countries and given aid not only in transportation and the working out of legal tangles, but also in food, clothing, medical care, pastoral services, and the meeting of every sort of human need. Through its subsidiary agencies such as Church World Service in America, many thousands of tons of food and clothing have been shipped every year to the victims of war and natural disasters in many parts of the world.

Another service rendered is through the Commission of the Churches on International Affairs, maintained in conjunction with the International Missionary Council. It works nonpolitically in close relation to the United Nations and has at times been able to give strategic counsel in situations of great tension, its influence unadvertised but not unfelt.

In its Division of Studies the W.C.C. has dealt not only with theological issues which might be beyond the grasp of most laymen, but with such pertinent problems as "The Meaning of Work," "The Evangelization of Man in Modern Mass Society," and "Our Common Christian Responsibility in Areas of Rapid Social Change." This division, like the Department on the Laity, issues a biennial bulletin.[3]

[3] Subscriptions to this bulletin, at 50 cents a year, may also be sent to World Council of Churches, Room 439, 475 Riverside Drive, New York 27, N.Y.

Turning to the complex and many-sided aspects of the work of the National Council of Churches, we shall attempt no more than to outline the range of its activities. Consisting as it does of the merged ecumenical activities of more than a dozen earlier bodies, it has a number of departments which reflect these formerly independent organizations. Among these are its Division of Christian Education, Division of Home Missions, Division of Foreign Missions, and Division of Christian Life and Work which carries forward much of what the Federal Council of Churches did before the merger in 1950. Other large enterprises are conducted through Church World Service, through the Central Department of Evangelism, through the Broadcasting and Film Commission, through the Bureau of Research and Survey, and through the Washington office which, though not engaged in political lobbying, keeps close watch on pending legislation and is a gold mine of information to the churches.

To narrate the activities of the various subdivisions of these many divisions, departments, and bureaus would extend this section to far too great length. The Division of Christian Life and Work may serve as a sample, and it is selected because its activities at so many points touch the concerns of the great majority of laymen. Its Department of International Affairs not only holds occasional nation-wide study conferences, but also keeps a long-range program of peace education and stimulus to action under way. The Department of the Church and Economic Life endeavors to secure the application of Christian principles to both the personal and the organizational aspects of business, industry, and agriculture. The Department of Racial and Cultural Relations engages in the field which its name indicates. Other departments supply counsel and guidance to hospital and prison chaplaincies; help to co-ordinate the health and welfare agencies of the churches with those of other voluntary and national agencies; and gather, analyze, and disseminate information on religious liberty. Every one of these activities deals with stewardship in the broader sense, but there is also within this division an agency which plans and promotes the annual United Stewardship Canvass with the aim of a more co-operative approach to self-support and benevolence giving in the churches.

A comparable list of activities could be mentioned for each of the other major divisions, but this is enough to indicate the wide range of concerns on which ecumenical leadership is available, and in which efforts are being made to help the churches to function more effectively through co-operation while each maintains its own identity.

But what of the ordinary local church layman in all this? With important exceptions, candor compels the observation that it almost passes him by.

To note the major exception, it is necessary to shift the pronoun from "him" to "her." The women of the Christian world have been praying together on the World Day of Prayer for the past seventy-five years. Since 1887 the first Friday in Lent has knit Christian women together in a great fellowship of prayer across national and denominational lines, long before most of us ever heard the word ecumenical. In 1940 the United Council of Church Women was formed. It dealt on a voluntary and not denominationally representative basis with many of the same concerns as the Federal Council of Churches, and was designed to unite the women of the churches for interdenominational worship, study, and action in their local communities. After serious soul searching as to whether affiliation might stifle autonomy, the decision was reached to merge with the National Council of Churches when the merger of numerous organizations was consummated in 1950.

The principal activities of the United Church Women are focused in three "first Fridays": the World Day of Prayer on the first Friday in Lent, now observed in nearly 150 countries around the world; the May Luncheon centering in local community problems on the first Friday in May; and the World Community Day on the first Friday in November, when attention is centered on world peace and service to the needy in a world Christian fellowship. Through its corresponding subdepartments, Christian World Missions, Christian Social Relations, and Christian World Relations, and the publication of its monthly journal, *The Church Woman,* ecumenical education and activity are continually being encouraged among large numbers of lay women in America.

In the National Council there is also a General Department of United Church Men. It aims to stir Christian laymen to a greater sense of their responsibility in such areas as Christian missions, support of Christian colleges, and better stewardship of money, time, and interest in their local churches and communities. It is not yet as active or as far-reaching in its effects as is the corresponding women's organization. Perhaps the women have more leisure; perhaps they are less bound by economic interests; perhaps they "take to church work" more readily. I will let the reader judge the reason.

There is a lay outreach toward ecumenicity in the Y.M.C.A.'s and Y.W.C.A.'s, not directly under the aegis of the Church but related to it and usually served and sponsored by lay Christians. There are also the national and world organizations of Christian students, with conferences, work camps, and other service projects which promote fellowship and obliterate distinctions. Long before there was a World Council of Churches, the World's Student Christian Federation was an organ of ecumenical fellowship and training in leadership, many of its present leaders having come to know and to love each other in that relationship.

Many thousands of foreign students come each year to the United States to study, not a few of whom are Christians. Their presence enlarges horizons and when fellowship is established, the reality of the world Christian community becomes more tangible.

So, to the statement that ecumenicity largely bypasses the grass roots there are significant exceptions. The exceptions for the most part follow an inherent logic, for ecumenicity came into being as a product of the missionary movement and at the lay level finds its most fertile soil in those areas where theological distinctions matter less than practical service—that is, among women, students, and youth.

3. LAYMEN'S INSTITUTES IN EUROPE

We come now to a movement which has made more headway in Europe than America, though it is beginning to make its impact in the United States. It is difficult to know what to call it, for it differs in different places. I have chosen the commonest title, but the institutes are not limited to laymen. Indeed, their genius lies in the fact that ministers, theologians, and specialists in the Bible along with laymen explore the implications of the Christian gospel for our time. They are also known as "evangelical academies," but they are usually not academies in the sense of offering an extended period of instruction, and while they are evangelical in the sense of being under Protestant auspices their primary purpose is not evangelism. Some are known as "communities," but the communal element is one of fellowship and common interest rather than living in the same location for an extended period. Walter M. Horton a few years ago wrote about those in Europe under the title, "Centers of New Life in European Christendom." A more recent booklet issued by the Department on the Laity of the World Council is entitled "Signs of Renewal." Put all of these terms together and one gets an apt description of them.

There are now about forty of these centers in Western Europe. We shall take a brief look at some of the best known, looking at them in the order of their founding.

1. *Sigtuna.* The earliest is the Sigtuna Foundation, dating from 1915, located in a charming, historic community between Stockholm and Uppsala in the east of Sweden. Its roots go back before the first world war to the "Young Church Movement" of the Swedish Student Christian Federation, which enlisted students to go out two by two into the parishes to try to relate the whole life of the people to God and the Church. The need was felt for a center for this work, and a man of far-seeing vision, Manfred (now Bishop) Björquist, took the lead in establishing the Foundation and served as its director for the first twenty-five years.

The buildings reflect the underlying philosophy of the Foundation. The Guest House provides accommodations for persons of many occupations, including a good many authors and artists, to work and relax in the secluded beauty of the place. It also houses conferences in which Christians, concerned secularists, and occasionally Communists find fellowship in an atmosphere of mutual exploration and good will. The Chapel gives a spiritual undergirding to the enterprise. A People's High School provides an opportunity for young adults to continue their education with literature, social studies, science, and history anchored in the Christian tradition. Although the American profession of Director of Religious Education is not found in Sweden—or elsewhere to my knowledge—the Lay Worker's Training College gives comparable preparation to parish workers. In short, the aim of Sigtuna is to bring the gospel to the secular world through fellowship, conference, worship, and study. It has appropriately been called a "watch-tower" and an "energizing center."

2. *Iona.* The second in sequence of time is doubtless more familiar to many readers, for much has been written about it. It is the Iona Community, centered during the summer months on the historic little island of Iona off the west coast of Scotland. It was founded in 1938 by the Rev. George MacLeod—now Sir

George, though characteristically he never uses the title—and he has remained its leader and central dynamo. As a minister of the Scotch Presbyterian Church, he served during the depression years in the industrial community of Govan, where he became convinced that the chasm between the clergy and the industrial worker could not be bridged until each had a chance to know each other's world, and that the Church could not serve the world in strength until this bridge was built in a "laboratory of living."

There were a number of reasons for the choice of Iona as the focus of this enterprise. First, there was the historic appropriateness of it. Columba with his little mission band of twelve men, only two of whom were ministers, landed there in A.D. 563, and from this center the gospel was spread to Scotland, Scandinavia, and other parts of Northern Europe. The work of the Church was then concerned with the whole of life, with agriculture and fishing, education and politics, as well as with the liturgy of the Church. The Celtic cross has a circle at its center which symbolizes the perfect union of the sacred and the secular, the spiritual and the material, this world and the next.

Furthermore, there was work at Iona that needed to be done. The ancient abbey and its environs had fallen into ruins, and while the Church of Scotland had rebuilt the church, the buildings about it where men had formerly lived and worked were collapsed and unusable. "This was symbolic of the state of Church and people. The Church building was in good repair, but the ordinary lives of men were in ruins." [4] The Iona Community, initially only four ministers and four artisans, was created to rebuild these structures during the summer months with a fellowship of manual labor, worship, and discussion, while during the other nine months the young ministers were to work at the task of rebuilding society with the gospel of

[4] Rev. Ralph Morton in "The Iona Community," *Professional Life as Christian Vocation* (Papers of the Ecumenical Institute, No. III), p. 59.

Christ, and the stonecutters and carpenters returned to their normal labors.

So it has continued. Ministers fresh from seminary have come to Iona, pledging two years of service on the island and the mainland, so that now the Community numbers 150 full members with a much larger number of Associates, ministers and laymen, men and women, who share in the disciplines and concerns of the community but without its summer activities. During the summer three days of each week are given to manual labor under the direction of skilled craftsmen, the rest to lectures, discussions, and study. Every morning and evening there are services of worship in the ancient twelfth-century abbey church where time melts into history and one feels the living reality of the communion of the saints. On Wednesday nights there are prayers of intercession for spiritual healing; on Thursday nights an Act of Belief in which any who desire, which generally includes many from the youth camps held also on the island, may make at the altar a dedication or rededication of life. By such acts the spiritual and the physical, work and worship, fellowship and prayer, are intermingled.

Less well known are the through-the-year activities of the Community. Its younger members serve usually under the guidance of a more experienced minister in a slum parish, an industrial housing development, an industrial chaplaincy, a youth center, or in some other setting that keeps them close to human need. Meanwhile they maintain a corporate discipline or "rule" of daily personal devotions and Bible study, planning of work time, and allocation of funds proportionate to income to causes mutually agreed upon by the Community.

It is apparent that the Iona Community stands for a very practical form of Christianity. Yet its basic foundation is the Incarnation. As our Lord became incarnate in human, material form, the entire material world and our total corporate life is potentially sacred. It is the aim of the Community to meet the challenge of secularism, not by withdrawing from the world, but by touching all of life with the service and the glory of the gospel.

The remaining centers to be described have all been founded since World War II, almost simultaneously at its close. In considerable measure they are the product of a concern which the war aroused in prophetic-spirited Christians.

3. *Bad Boll.* The Evangelical Academy at Bad Boll, near Stuttgart, began to function in September, 1945. It is now the headquarters of the eighteen similar academies in Germany and is the prototype of many others. It is so called from the original use of the term "Academy" in Plato's time as a place of informal conversation and a common search for answers to life's basic questions.

During the war Eberhard Müller, the present director of Bad Boll, and Helmut Thielicke, now professor of theology at Hamburg, became deeply concerned over the divorce between German Protestantism and the actual problems of the world. Why did not the Church take a stronger stand against National Socialism? Why were so many people, especially the intellectuals and workers, estranged from the Church? Why was theology so abstract, the province of the clergy but fenced off from the laymen? In addition to such general questions they found a deep unrest among various occupational groups—lawyers, doctors, teachers, economists, soldiers—who found their old moorings gone but with no clear sense of purpose to replace them.

The answer came in the resolution to establish a Protestant academy which would be a meeting ground where people of different occupations could discuss their everyday problems of belief and action with representatives of the Church in an atmosphere of informality and freedom.

Accordingly, the primary function of Bad Boll is to provide such a conference center, with the group usually having a common vocational concern. The "spectrum" of the hundreds of week-end or longer conferences which have been held there, listed in a descriptive booklet, indicates the wide variety of occupations and interests—mayors, soldiers, refugees, teachers, students, high-school graduates, doctors, midwives, nurses, war widows, housewives, secretaries, women workers, salesmen, industrial social workers, other social workers, leading manufacturers, industrial workers, young workers, apprentices, craftsmen, farmers, young farmers, pastors, pastors' wives, laymen in industry, youth workers, the younger generation.

Many who attend are not Christians but are drawn by a sense of the worth of the interchange. There are voluntary worship services and a period of Bible study, purposely kept informal to embarrass no one. The primary part of the day's activities, however, consists of an introductory lecture or panel, often with representatives of both the Church and the occupational group speaking, and then a free-for-all discussion of basic problems in the field. The method has met with such favor that now most of the invitations are extended through industrial firms and professional associations. Employers sometimes release time and defray expenses for their workers to attend.

The philosophy of the Evangelical Academies is that the best evangelism is not that which attempts to entice persons into the Church, but that which demonstrates the relevancy of the message of the Church to all of life. Dr. Müller thus graphically expresses it:

> It is extremely hard to draw non-churchmen into groups which bear a particularly "religious" stamp. . . . The missionary work of the Protestant Academy, then, does not use the fishing-rod to extract individual souls from the pond of the world and bring them into a Christian environment. It uses a net which catches "all sorts and all sizes." . . . Where the message of the Word of God is linked with a completely open-minded approach to men of this world and to their problems, it should be possible to avoid the Church becoming either

secularized and worldly, or on the other hand degenerating into a ghetto of the pious.[5]

4. *Kerk en Wereld.* A project with a similar purpose but a different structure came into being in November, 1945. This is *Kerk en Wereld* (Church and World) at Driebergen near Utrecht in central Holland.

This was born out of the agony of Nazi occupation. It owes its origin chiefly to Dr. Kraemer, who saw the urgent necessity of the revitalization of the Dutch Reformed Church, and to Philip Eykman who died for his faith in Buchenwald but had managed to pass on to his fellow prisoners his vision of a Church serving the world in every aspect of secular life. Immediately at the close of the war in 1945 a large estate was purchased with church funds accumulated but unspent during the occupation, and *Kerk en Wereld* was launched. Four years later a conference center, the Eykman House, was opened near by as the gift of the Presbyterian Church, U.S.A.

The primary note in *Kerk en Wereld* is the preparation of laymen for Christian service in the world. This takes the form of a four-year course—three years in residence—to train young men and women as youth workers, social workers, industrial personnel managers, and other forms of professional lay service. These are called Wikas, WIKA being the initials of the Dutch words for "workers in church-sponsored activities." For two years the Wikas pursue a curriculum of Bible study, Christian faith and ethics, psychology, social studies, and the specialized skills of their chosen line of work. The third year is spent in an interneship under supervision. The fourth year they return for more theological training and a concentrated emphasis on evangelism.

At Eykman House numerous conferences similar to those

[5] *Signs of Renewal,* Department on the Laity, World Council of Churches, p. 10. Used by permission.

at Bad Boll are held for week ends or longer periods. A distinctive feature is the giving of week-end courses for laymen, extending at intervals through the year, in Bible study, essentials of the Church, modes of evangelism, and personal and social ethics. Other long-range courses are designed for personnel managers in large industries to help them put human relations on a spiritual foundation.

Thus the work at *Kerk en Wereld* is more specifically evangelistic and church-centered than that at Bad Boll, but both are vital attempts to bring the light of the Christian faith to bear on the secular world through the concerned and informed activity of laymen.

Each of the four institutions we have visited is under the aegis of a particular state church. We now look at one which is ecumenical and international and which correlates the work of these and many other less famous centers.

5. *The Ecumenical Institute, Chateau de Bossey.* At Celigny, some fifteen miles out from Geneva and in a lovely setting overlooking the lake, is an eighteenth-century chateau with a twelfth-century tower which houses the Ecumenical Institute of the World Council of Churches. This long past is symbolic of its rootage, yet it is very contemporary and forward-looking in its activities and program. It too owes much to the vision of Dr. Hendrik Kraemer, its initiator and first director, while the building in which it is housed is the gift of another great Christian layman, John D. Rockefeller, Jr.

The Institute opened its doors in October, 1946, its first group being composed of many who had suffered in concentration camps, worked in the underground, and felt acutely the separations as well as the other privations of war. From the beginning such fellowship across national boundaries has enriched its life and thought. Within flexible limits it follows a rather definite pattern of activities.

Common to all types of groups meeting at Bossey are worship

and daily Bible study. This is more than an incidental adjunct to discussion, for the Institute proceeds on the assumption that all ecumenical work should be grounded in listening to the Word of God as this is found to bear on the contemporary problems of the world.

With this common center the work of the Institute follows four main lines. One of these is the holding of vocational conferences similar to those we have seen elsewhere, but with the difference that they are international in personnel, there are fewer of them, they last longer (usually five days to a week), and their members are drawn more largely from leaders in their respective fields.

There are teaching courses of from ten days to three weeks for laymen, for theological students, for missionaries on furlough, and for pastors who come to Bossey to learn about the aims of the ecumenical movement and its bearing on their work.

There are the research consultations of the World Council itself. Its various departments must bring together, often for several days at a time, the Commission members dealing with special studies. A number of such studies are in process continually; Bossey is their usual meeting-place.

There is a Graduate School of Ecumenical Studies. This is an advanced study course for seminary graduates or those of equivalent maturity, held in conjunction with the University of Geneva through its theological faculty. It deals with the history of the ecumenical movement, issues of ecclesiology involved in it, particular charactistics of the denominations, the social and ethical problems confronting churches today, the movements of renewal now going forward in it—such matters as we have had occasion to look at in this book. It is easy to foresee that those who pursue such study in an international fellowship will be better leaders of their own churches, to say nothing of more informed participants in the ecumenical movement, in the years to come.

Here we must stop, as far as Europe is concerned. Nothing has been said about the other lay institutes of Sweden, Germany, the Netherlands, and Switzerland; those of Finland and France; the great *Kirchentag* assemblies of hundreds of thousands of German laymen; the "Kirk Week" and "Tell Scotland" movements of that country; the special studies for laymen available in five Y.M.C.A. colleges and a number of other Christian colleges in England; the Agape youth movement in Italy; the Zoe movement in Greece.[6] Enough has been said to indicate that signs of renewal are stirring in Europe and that in spite of—or perhaps because of—the sterility of much of European church life, laymen are on the march.

What of signs of advance in America? To these we must turn in another chapter.

[6] Brief accounts of most of these movements are to be found in the booklet, *Signs of Renewal*. For a survey of important projects in evangelism, which include a number of these, see also the Amsterdam volume, *Man's Disorder and God's Design*, section II, pp. 113-67. For a more extensive description and interpretation, Margaret Frakes, *Bridges to Understanding* (Philadelphia: Muhlenberg Press, 1960), is very valuable.

Chapter VIII

MORE SIGNS OF ADVANCE

THIS CHAPTER IS A CONTINUATION OF THE PRECEDING, FOR EVEN AN abbreviated account of what the ecumenical movement and the laymen's institutes of Europe are doing in reference to our theme took all its space. In this one we shall center more largely on the American scene, though so interrelated is our world today, including the church world, that to speak of what is happening in one area is by implication to suggest effects in others.

We shall begin by looking at a few American centers of lay training and fellowship which bear some resemblance to the European laymen's institutes. Without being an exact parallel, these are in part adaptations of the European pattern, in part an indigenous development.

1. AMERICAN LAY CENTERS

The idea of an evangelical academy or lay training center has not made the headway in America that it has in Europe. Whether judged by popular interest, attendance, or financial support, those that have been attempted seem in general less flourishing. Those that exist are not widely known; in fact, many American Christians know more about the European centers than about those nearer to them. Is it because we care less? Because they have not been in operation long enough for the public to get on to the idea? Because we are too preoccupied with other things? Probably some of each. Before we give way to self-condemnation or discouragement, however, some important sociological facts need to be considered.

As one factor, we have noticed how the German academies, the Dutch *Kerk en Wereld* at Driebergen, and many not specifically described were the direct result of the social as well as physical destructiveness of war and the shattering of long-established social patterns. Something had to be done if either church or world was to survive with any health. By comparison America was in the war but not of it.

As another factor, American church life has maintained a far higher degree of community respect, proportionate church attendance, and lay participation in its manifold organizations and activities, than has been or is yet the case in Europe. In spite of much that can be said about the shallowness of the recent revival of religion in America, with laments either sad or scornful over our "pseudo-Christianity" and "post-Protestant" culture, the fact remains that great numbers of American Protestant Christians love their church and devote to it large amounts of money, time, and talent. This does not mean that we are doing enough or are as true to the essential nature of the Church as we ought to be—Chapter V gave plenty of evidence to the contrary. Yet without grounds for boastfulness, American Christians can humbly thank God for the residual health still evident in our churches.

Another marked difference is the focusing of strength within denominations in a pluralistic society. Four of the five institutes looked at in the previous chapter speak to the nation from the vantage point of a largely homogenous Protestantism, while the fifth takes its stance from the prestige of the World Council of Churches. In America there are strong denominations and strong lay activities geared to the internal concerns of these denominations, but none that speaks to or for our society as a whole. The National Council in a measure speaks for Protestantism, but only "in a measure." If we are to have such

Protestant lay centers they must either be sponsored by a denomination, sponsored by the National Council of Churches, or inaugurated and maintained by a local ecumenical group. Since the financial and other hazards are considerable in the last instance we may add a fourth possibility—to be underwritten by one or more of the large foundations.

While the National Council has done much to create and disseminate interest in the work of the laity, it has no center comparable to the Chateau de Bossey. Beginnings have been made under the fourth alternative, but except for such outstanding contributions as the Danforth and Rockefeller Foundations have made to student work, extensive support for lay centers must yet be awaited. Most of what we can report falls under the first or third possibility.

These centers are of various types, and the types merge into each other without clear delineation. Judgments as to relative importance must necessarily be subjective. We shall look at a few which may serve as illustrative and suggestive.

1. *Denominational centers.* Practically every major denomination owns one or more retreat centers, usually in the midst of beautiful surroundings, with accommodations for guests, a chapel, and a meeting room where conferences are held. Some of these are national, others regional. Memories and deep emotions often cluster about them. To speak of Lake Junaluska to Methodists, of Green Lake to American Baptists, of Ridgecrest to Southern Baptists, or of Montreat to Southern Presbyterians is to do more than speak a name; it is to call up a constellation of friendships, activities, and moments of depth and power.

It is not with these centers and their conferences that we are primarily concerned here, for while laymen as well as clergy attend them, they seldom focus on examining the status and service of the laity as the Church within the world. Often there is concern for the work of the laity within the Church; such gatherings do not a little to stimulate the lay persons who attend them to give more of their time and energy to the Church. This is good, but if the thesis of this book is correct, it is not enough.

It is of some significance that the oldest and perhaps the best known of the American lay training centers was founded under the auspices of a denomination which historically has only laymen in it, and which from its beginnings has been concerned about the social applications of the gospel. This is Pendle Hill at Wallingford, Pennsylvania, established by the Quakers in 1930 with Henry Hodgkin, a distinguished English Friend, as its inaugurator and first director.

Pendle Hill combines a year-round, noncredit study center with a place for holding theme conferences and spiritual retreats. It brings together for meditation, fellowship, and serious but largely unpatterned study Christians of many denominations, possibly half of whom at any particular time may be Quakers. Usually there are foreign students and a few Negroes in the group. Everybody who comes participates in the household and maintenance chores, partly as a matter of basic philosophy regarding the importance of manual labor to spiritual enrichment and fellowship, but also as a practical means of maintaining the institution on slender resources.

The Pendle Hill approach, as might be expected of a Quaker center, makes much of the "inner light" and of quiet listening to the Christ Within. Yet this signifies no introverted withdrawal from the world. It is deeply concerned with the outward expressions of the gospel, essentially from the standpoint of reconciling love. Its courses and conferences characteristically deal not only with Quaker history, the devotional life, and the Bible, but also with international peacemaking, modern industrial problems, and other aspects of the individual's relation to his community. The strength of Pendle Hill lies in both the breadth and depth of its approach; its limitation in the fact that Quakerism, though widely respected and influential beyond its numbers, lies somewhat outside the main stream of American denominational life.

The center in America which most closely resembles the European pattern, having drawn much of its inspiration from Driebergen, Bad Boll, Bossey, and Iona, is Parishfield in a rural setting near Brighton, Michigan. This is under Protestant Episcopal auspices. Established in 1948, its property is owned by the Diocese of Michigan and its resident members are Episcopalians, but it reaches out on an ecumenical basis to serve any who desire to come. It is named Parishfield because it aims both to be a parish and to assist parishes in the renewal of church life in service to the world.

Since it has experimented from time to time with various procedures, its program cannot be described in a fixed form. Certain common factors, however, run through it. Its major service is in week-end or through-the-week conferences, sometimes of parish groups concerned with the revivification of their church, sometimes of laity or of laity and clergy together on the basis of vocational groups or of major issues in the outreach of the Church to the world. Group Bible study every morning is basic procedure, on the conviction that the problems of the world should be approached by Christians on the foundation of a quest for light from the Word of God. The normal program of the day includes also two periods of discussion; a period of manual labor; and a time for recreation, corporate worship, and family prayers.

In recent years a growing number of lay men and women and some ordained ministers who have seen a fresh vision at Parishfield have banded together as "partners for renewal" and have committed themselves to particular programs of study and action in society, such as the correction and prevention of crime, university education, television, and politics.

2. *Ecumenical centers.* These two must suffice as examples of

projects denominationally sponsored. We shall now look at two others brought into being by local ecumenical initiative.

The Ecumenical Institute at Evanston, Illinois, doubtless owed its origin in part, though not wholly, to the interest created by the holding of the World Council's Second Assembly in that city in 1954. The pattern differs from the others outlined in that many of its conferences have been held on a one-day basis, drawing attendance from the surrounding area. In most cases an expert in the field under consideration has presented the issues—thus conforming to the prevalent American desire to hear a speaker—with discussion following. The topics for attention, as in the European institutes, have covered a wide range of vocational and social interests, with occasional consultations on local ecumenicity and other matters directly related to the ecumenical movement. There have also been a number of sequences of evening lectures, mainly on theological topics.

This is an important undertaking, geared to the pattern of urban and suburban living with its many competing interests. Yet problems have emerged. For one thing, the brevity of the sessions was a barrier. A day or an evening can arouse interest; it is hardly long enough to let the interest deepen, the fellowship ripen, and new insights be crystallized into action. For another, the participants in conferences from the various vocations and disciplines have often lacked a sufficient grounding in the Christian faith to have really fruitful encounters. The pattern is shifting, therefore, to a more intensive and long-range study program.

Among the most vigorous of the American lay centers is the Christian Faith and Life Community adjacent to the University of Texas at Austin. Here continuity is provided by the fact that its central core of participants is made up of students at the University, living, worshiping, and studying together. Living at the residence houses of the Community, they covenant for a year to maintain a corporate discipline and, in addition to their regular University work, to pursue a course of study in theology, Bible studies, church history, and Christian ethics. The taking of such courses in the late evening when all are free plus the required reading and tutorial seminars is demanding enough to rule out all but the genuinely committed. This program brings together young people of various races, national backgrounds, and vocational objectives for a common serious pursuit of the implications of Christian faith for life in today's world. It should make a marked difference in the leadership these same young persons will give to the Church in the years ahead.

In the Austin Community, besides these studies at the College House, there is also a Laos House for the training of laymen. Here "laic theological studies" are available in both evening and week-end courses. Parish ministers' colloquies are also held here to consider the world-wide angles of the renewal of the Church in relation to the life and mission of the local church. A recent development is the campus ministers' symposium.

In each of the last two projects surveyed we noticed a serious concern for the theological education of the laity. This leads us to look at a further sign of advance.

2. LAY THEOLOGY

One of the most important movements of the mid-twentieth century is the emergence of a concern by laymen for a better understanding of the foundations of their faith, and correlative with this the writing of books and the providing of courses of instruction to make this understanding possible.

This is related to what has been happening in the ranks of the theologians. Theology today is in a more virile state than it has been in for a long time. The ultraconservative biblical literalism that is generally termed "fundamentalism" was supplanted among the scholars fifty to seventy-five years ago by a historical approach to the Bible and a spirit of free inquiry that largely bridged the gap between religion and science and put a strong accent on the social gospel. This liberalism, though decried by some as lacking in evangelistic fervor, did a great deal of good in making it possible for mind and heart to work together to believe and to serve in the spirit of Jesus. It sometimes went too far, however, in understressing the sinfulness of man, the uniqueness of Jesus Christ as the one Savior of mankind, and the transcendent holiness of God. It was inevitable that there should be a swing back more nearly to the center.

This corrective came in the emergence in America in the 1930's and 1940's (earlier in Europe) of what is variously termed neo-orthodoxy, the new Reformation theology, or less correctly Barthianism from its first and most famous exponent, Karl Barth. Reinhold Niebuhr became its foremost exponent in the United States, and for years he rang the changes on the defects of liberalism, particularly with regard to its overestimate of man's goodness and expectations of social progress, but also on many other matters in which he believed that liberalism had conformed too much to secular standards of philosophy and morality. Yet he himself had been trained in the liberal historical approach to the Bible and was deeply committed to the Christian obligation to challenge the evils of society. These he could not surrender, and this has continued to be true of most of the great neo-orthodox theologians, although some of their lesser followers have let the emphasis on man's sin and weakness curtail the impulse to social action.[1]

We stand now in somewhat of a "middle ground" position. There are, of course, wide differences among contemporary theologians—enough points of view to keep debate interesting

[1] In the past this concern for social action was much more marked among American than among European theologians, but under the crisis of the times and the influence of ecumenical conversation a considerable regard for what is now usually termed "the responsible society" has emerged in Europe.

and fruitful. Yet there is far more agreement than difference, partly as a result of the meeting of minds in ecumenical encounters, probably more because the seriousness of the times in conjunction with serious scholarship has caused a sloughing off of extremes and a coming toward the center to find a dimension of depth. Biblical theology is dominant, and on this basis both the sinfulness and the dignity of man, the reality of judgment and the hope of redemption, the uniqueness of the revelation of God in Jesus Christ and the possibility of Christian experience and social action through the grace of God, are defended. I can here only hint at the nature of these trends, but there are excellent books in which one can pursue them.[2]

What of the layman in this? Has he turned theologian? The layman has always been reaching out, often without realizing it, for a theology, for all the ultimate questions of life are theological. When bereavement occurs or some other deep suffering befalls him he almost spontaneously asks, "Why did this happen?" When his loved ones die, his faith in eternal life has slight foundation unless it is grounded in the goodness of God who loves us for time and eternity. In smoother times, if he finds meaning and purpose in life, it is through belief in the goodness and power of the Creator who has given us this kind of world in which to live and labor. If he worships and prays in a vital way he needs to know that he is praying to a personal God who can hear and respond. In his manifold ethical decisions—though he may make them without thinking of his religion, and too often he does—if he tries to be Christian he must think of Christ and of what Christ tells us of the will of God.

In recent years both theologians and laymen have come to

[2] Among the best are Daniel Day Williams' *What Present-Day Theologians Are Thinking* (rev. ed. New York: Harper & Brothers, 1959); William Hordern's *A Layman's Guide to Protestant Theology* (New York: The Macmillan Company, 1955); and L. Harold DeWolf's *Present Trends in Christian Thought* (New York: Association Press, 1960).

an awareness of this need of theology by all. Twenty years ago there were scarcely a half dozen books of theology in print to which a layman of ordinary intelligence and education could turn. Now there are many of them, some in series such as the "Layman's Theological Library" (The Westminster Press) or the "Know Your Faith Series" (Abingdon Press), others by numerous authors. The Interpreter's Bible is a mammoth twelve-volume project published by Abingdon Press from which a layman can glean much theology as well as biblical knowledge. His church library should have it. While theologians, like scientists, write primarily for those who already are professionals in the field, it is no longer true that a Christian layman lacks tools for the study of his faith if he is alert to its importance.

The books are available. But what of the stimulus to use them? Books are most often fruitful in personal encounter, where there can be discussion of their content and where people are free within a fellowship to agree or disagree with the book and with each other. This suggests the need of classes and forums for discussion.

This too is a need on the way to being met. The church-school curricula, even for children, are more theologically oriented than they formerly were, and if kept to the degree of the maturity of the child, important foundations can be laid here. Children wrestle with deeper questions than adults often give them credit for, and they merit as full and frank an answer as can be given. The youth fellowship groups, the adult division of the church school, the church family night, the woman's society or the men's club meetings, to say nothing of special discussion groups oriented about this particular purpose, are fruitful media for transmitting a better understanding of biblical faith and its bearing on the problems of our world.

What of a layman's school of religion, comparable to a theological seminary but geared to the interests, needs, and maturity of laymen? In a number of centers this has passed from the dream stage and has become a reality. It takes various forms. For many years there have been community-wide schools of leadership training usually sponsored by the local Council of Churches and intended mainly for the training of church-school teachers. In them there has almost always been biblical content and of late more theological emphasis. They serve a very useful purpose and should be supported. What is emerging now is not a replica of these, but a type of laymen's school which centers around the studies usually found in a theological curriculum. The school is designed not for embryo clergy or essentially for church-school teachers but for any laymen who want to learn and will pay the price of serious study.

The most ambitious laymen's school of religion is the one that is centered in Berkeley, California. So far as is known, it is the most extensive, systematic study process offered to laymen in the world. It owes its origin chiefly to the initiative of Mrs. Muriel James, who is an ordained Congregational minister. She, together with the presidents and deans of four seminaries in the Bay Area and several laymen, pastors, and professors, established the school in the fall of 1959. Most of the faculty is drawn from seminaries of the vicinity—the Pacific School of Religion (interdenominational), the Berkeley Baptist Divinity School (American Baptist), the Church Divinity School of the Pacific (Protestant Episcopal), the San Francisco Theological Seminary (Presbyterian), and the Pacific Lutheran Seminary.

Though centered in Berkeley, the school very early began to reach out to establish a number of neighboring branches in order to bring instruction to where the people live. It has continued to grow in strength, with a carefully integrated curriculum of studies in the Bible, church history, Christian theology, and Christian ethics. There are four six-week quarters a year, each class meeting two hours a week with required reading and papers. The curriculum is under constant scrutiny and revision by a committee of professors, clergy, and lay people. In its second year several courses designed for the resident clergy of the area were added to those being offered to the laity. Tuition fees, purposely kept low to increase the availability of the courses to persons of moderate means, have financed about one third of the program, the remaining costs being cared for by individual donors, interested local churches and several denominations, with some help from foundations.

Other theological courses for laymen have been offered by the Chicago Theological Seminary, the Lancaster and the Eden Seminaries of the United Church of Christ, and other schools. There is no special pattern to follow, for local circumstances call for a program adapted to the situation. To judge from the number of inquiries that have come to the Laymen's School of Religion in Berkeley as to organization and curriculum there is a widespread interest in the establishment of more such schools.[3] The laymen's desire to be better informed about their faith and the leaders' desire to provide the opportunity are unmistakably signs of advance.

3. TOWARD A DEEPER DEVOTIONAL LIFE

A concern for deepening the devotional life can hardly be said to be new. Christians of every country—indeed, the religious of all faiths and of all lands and times—have prayed. Religion centers in the worship of God or of many gods, and at least in the high religions it is recognized that personal as well as corporate worship is essential to the life of the spirit. Yet today we seem too busy, with too many other things to do. Furthermore, in the mind of the sophisticated modern who has not been sufficiently instructed in theology, there is often a lurking suspicion that prayer for oneself partakes of magic

[3] For further information about the Berkeley Laymen's School of Religion see the article by Edward S. Setchko, "Toward an Informed Laity," *The Christian Century,* LXXVII, No. 20 (May 18, 1960), 603-4.

and prayer for others of incantation, with the whole process simply a form of self-hypnosis and autosuggestion.

Nevertheless, over the past few years there has been a decided upturn of interest in, and presumably of the practice of, the devotional life. What John Casteel in the title of one of the best books on the subject calls "rediscovering prayer" has begun. We shall note some of the evidences in a moment, but first let us look at the reasons why.

The most obvious reason is the miasma of fear, suspicion, inner and outer pressure, insecurity, and tension that engulfs many lives. There are the usual tragedies that beset human existence, alleviated to some extent by better medical care and more safety devices, but intensified at other points by more complex and dangerous living. Along with these there is a suffocating cloud of apprehension about the state of the world, and perhaps about one's own finances or job or family. Such conditions do not automatically generate a practice of prayer, but if one has in him a residual faith in God and belief in prayer, he is apt to feel with the Negro spiritual:

> It's me, O Lawd,
> A-standin' in the need of prayer.

Another causal factor is the psychological bill of health which prayer has received of late, not only from preachers and psychiatrists but also from journalists and popular writers. This is good but it is also dangerous. The danger lies in the possibility that the preachers may flee from social action to the less controversial terrain of the inner life; that the psychiatrist—and even some preachers—may treat prayer as a therapeutic device rather than a reverent and committed centering of life upon God and His holy will; that the journalists and other popular writers may be too naïve in their theology. Nevertheless, prayer is receiving enough salesmanship in these days to forestall some of the intellectual questioning of a generation ago and to relieve embarrassment at admitting an interest in it or the practice of it.

A third reason for increased concern is also an evidence of concern. This is the production and extensive sale of a considerable number of excellent devotional manuals and books about prayer. How widely they are used no one knows, but at least they are bought. To this may be added the phenomenal sales of the Methodist *Upper Room,* the Presbyterian *Today,* the Episcopalian *Forward,* and other periodical devotional booklets.

A fourth factor is the emergence of experimental groups, retreats, and schools of prayer. These are quite closely related to the various types of laymen's centers at which we have been looking in this and the previous chapter, yet they have certain distinctive features.

We shall begin with the prayer groups in local churches, though these groups are often the product of a movement elsewhere. Sometimes they are denominationally sponsored, as, for example, by the Spiritual Life Committee of the Woman's Society of Christian Service. Sometimes those who have attended a conference, ashram, or retreat and have been deeply moved by this experience wish to stay together for periodic corporate prayer. Sometimes it is a cell group started by two or three who ask others to join them and ideally—though less often actually—subdivide when the number reaches ten or twelve. Sometimes it is a local unit of such a semi-structured national redemptive fellowship as the Disciplined Order of Christ or the Yokefellow Associates. Sometimes a prayer group, affiliated with others of a similar nature, is organized and supervised by a person who makes this his main business, and who may receive pay for his supervision and counsel.

Good can come out of any of these procedures, provided the group is centered in a humble, open-spirited listening to the Holy Spirit and a committed willingness to discover and do the will of God in daily life. On the whole, the less professional and the less psychologically oriented such a group is, the more vital it is apt to be. This is not to discourage professional wisdom or psychology, and doubtless many have been helped by a prayer therapy such as is set forth in a book like William Parker's *Prayer Can Change Your Life.*[4] Yet the focus of attention is all-important, and it is basic to the Christian outlook as compared with the therapeutic that attention be centered, not on oneself, but on God and His will and on the love and service of other persons in the way of Christ.

Such locally established and continuing prayer groups have in them a great potential for sweeping away both social and ecclesiastical distinctions and uniting laity and clergy in a common quest for God. The idea of them is old; they go back to the twelve in the upper room and to those of whom it is written that after Pentecost "day by day, attending the temple together and breaking bread in their homes, they partook of food with glad and generous hearts, praising God and having favor with all the people" (Acts 2:46-47). As now conducted they are a relatively new development. There are perils in them; the danger of developing a "holier-than-thou" attitude and of making the group, rather than the Church, the beloved *koinonia* are ever present. Whether this group devotional experience becomes a private luxury or a conscience-quickened and spiritually deepened instrument of public service depends on the group's willingness to listen as God speaks.

Another movement which is old yet new is the occasional retreat for the deepening of the spiritual life. We saw elements of this at Pendle Hill and Parishfield, but it merits some analysis of its own.

Everybody needs at times to leave the pressure of his ordinary activities and the routine of daily living to be alone with God,

[4] William R. Parker and Elaine St. Johns (Englewood Cliffs, N. J.: Prentice-Hall, Inc., 1957).

or alone in the company of others of kindred mind. Personal and private devotions, fellowship groups like those just described, or the Sunday service of worship in the church sanctuary may afford such temporary withdrawal. Yet a further means of withdrawal for spiritual renewal can be a most helpful supplement to any of these, and may leave one with the feeling which William Wordsworth expressed in lines of classic beauty:

> I have felt
> A presence that disturbs me with the joy
> Of elevated thoughts; a sense sublime
> Of something far more deeply interfused,
> Whose dwelling is the light of setting suns,
> And the round ocean and the living air,
> And the blue sky, and in the mind of man.[5]

As an essential part of it, let us not forget certain other lines from the same poem:

> But hearing oftentimes
> The still, sad music of humanity.

We know from the New Testament that Jesus often withdrew from the multitude to pray, and in his taking of Peter, James, and John up to the Mount of Transfiguration and into the Garden, the precedent for corporate retreat is established. The Roman Catholic Church has long had such possibilities of withdrawal, not only in its permanent Orders, but also in temporary groups. Among Protestants the Anglicans—in this country the Episcopalians—have been pioneers in this field, often opening the houses of their Orders and providing leadership from them, at other times holding the retreats in church houses used for various purposes. Of late the retreat movement has assumed importance in most of the major Protestant denom-

[5] From "Lines Composed a Few Miles Above Tintern Abbey."

inations, and retreat centers in the midst of beautiful, secluded surroundings are becoming more and more numerous.

There is no single pattern, but the retreat lasts usually from one day to a week, with the week end from Friday evening to Sunday afternoon as the norm. There is usually some instruction by a leader, and long periods of silence for private devotional reading and meditation. Some and perhaps all meals are eaten in silence, broken only by the leader's reading aloud from *The Imitation of Christ,* Thomas Kelly's *A Testament of Devotion,* the writings of Evelyn Underhill, or some other pertinent counsel on the spiritual life. Both because long-continued silence is so unnatural to most Americans of today as to become oppressive and because fellowship is also contributory to Christian development, the retreat normally provides for coffee breaks or for tea and conversation. Sometimes also, varying with the constituency of the group, there is provision for organized recreation. Time is nearly always provided for serious general discussion of spiritual concerns, personal testimony, and the sharing of experience. Corporate worship at the beginning and at intervals during the retreat unites the group, and it not uncommonly comes to its conclusion and climax in the Lord's Supper.

The surroundings in which such retreats are held should be simple as well as secluded, but life at the retreat house is seldom ascetic, unless a sacrificial meal is engaged in as a reminder of the need to reach out in service to the hungry. Not mortification of the flesh, but rededication of the spirit, is the major note.

The retreat for a deeper fellowship with God and with one another has become a relatively common practice in American church life. It should be clear, however, that a gathering for much conversation, a church planning session, a business conference, or a school for instruction in leadership techniques or even in theology is not a retreat in the true sense of the word.

It may fulfill an important purpose and at another time be held at the same place, but a retreat exists for silent listening to God, not for much speaking.

Of the many retreat centers in the United States, among the best known are Pendle Hill, Parishfield, and Kirkridge in the Pocono mountains near Bangor, Pennsylvania. Having already seen something of the first two, we shall conclude this section with a look at Kirkridge.

Kirkridge was founded in 1942 by a group of men, mainly Presbyterians, who were captured by the idea of the Iona Community and felt the need of something comparable in America which might unite a devotional discipline and fellowship with the application of the gospel in a relevant way to the needs of our times. A 350-acre tract, mostly mountain woodland, was secured, and an old farmhouse supplemented by a modern lodge was made available for guests, much of the work being done by those coming to Kirkridge for retreat.

One purpose of Kirkridge is to provide a meeting place for such retreat groups as have just been described. On most week ends and many days in between it is thus occupied, the group bringing its own leadership and paying for the use of the facilities.

Yet it has a deeper purpose. This is the uniting of those who have the desire and intention in a Protestant "rule." This rule centers in a spiritual discipline but reaches out to quicken action at many points where Christian faith meets modern culture: barriers of communication, social injustices, international order, art forms, liturgy, psychology, theology. The needs and possibilities of social change are placed within the framework of personal spiritual commitment.

There is no Kirkridge "membership" but there is now a considerable number of persons who keep the Kirkridge Discipline, without external compulsion but as they are able to maintain it. These persons, ministers and laymen, men and women of a dozen or more denominations, come together if possible at least once a year at Kirkridge for retreat. The major part of the discipline goes on at home, however. Those who undertake it declare their intention to devote at least a half hour daily to private devotions with the use of a common lectionary; to identify in specific ways with suffering persons; to keep the mind alert by reading at least one solid book each month; to discipline time, energy, and money in Christian stewardship; to assume responsibility in the life and work of a local congregation; to meet with a few others regularly in a group for spiritual nurture. In addition to the annual Kirkridge group retreat, provision is made for a personal retreat of at least two hours each month, alone with God and in silence, in order to gain Christian perspective and to review and renew one's priorities of commitment.

Difficult? There is nothing here that the busiest Christian could not find time for and profit from. Yet it is more than many Christians, including many Christian leaders, do. The lack of such spiritual discipline on the part of both ministers and laymen may well be a major cause of the shallowness and secularism of our churches.

4. RELIGION AND THE ARTS

Another movement coming into prominence in America, less patterned as to places and centers, more diffused among Christian leaders and gradually engaging the attention of the laity, is the connection between Christianity and the arts.

There is, in the first place, a new interest in the ecclesiastical arts—church music, church architecture, drama in the church, liturgy, and related matters. This interest stems from a fresh appreciation of the importance of symbolism in the apprehension and communication of religious meanings. Some would follow Paul Tillich in making theology itself center in symbolic but nonliteral statements of religious truth; nearly everybody would grant the importance of symbols, whether of words or forms, to the intuitive and feeling aspects of religious faith. It is in its power to call forth deep emotions through an appeal to deeper levels than the intellect that art has its power, and rightly used, it can increase the love of God and neighbor.

Church music and liturgics have long had a place in the curriculum of theological seminaries as contributory to worship, but are coming into fresh importance as the long, great heritage of the past in these fields is seen both to yield treasures for contemporary life and to call for experimentation in new forms. The experimentation can be pushed too far—I am not yet convinced that putting the Lord's Supper into jazz is appropriate! Yet kept within the bounds of authentic worship and good taste, corporate worship can be greatly enriched by artistry in sacred music and the liturgy.

Likewise, as expressions of religious feeling and the communication of religious meanings, new developments in church architecture, religious drama, and the use of the voice in speech and of the body in the dance are claiming attention. No blanket praise or condemnation can be expressed. It all depends! Some of the newer churches, I must say, strike me as monstrosities, while others without being merely a replica of the past are conventional enough to be both worshipful and beautiful. An artistic and meaningful rendering of Alan Paton's *Cry the Beloved Country* in the form of the musical opera *Lost in the Stars,* of Christopher Fry's *A Sleep of Prisoners,* or of W. H. Auden's *For the Time Being* can drive home the message of the Christian faith with deep effectiveness. So, too, can great passages in the Bible be expressed, not only gracefully, but also in their deeper meaning *graciously* in the rhythm of choral speaking or bodily movement.

The production and rendition of art in the fields just mentioned, including church music, is usually the work of laymen. This fact points, on the one hand, to the great contributions that can be made by laity skilled in these arts. To do such work and to do it well is a Christian calling of equal significance with the clerical ministry. And, on the other hand, it suggests that these laymen, as much as clergy, must understand the message of the gospel and have along with their technical skills a knowledge of the Christian faith.

A somewhat different area of convergence of interest between religion and the arts is found in what contemporary literature, painting, sculpture, and secular drama, together with the movies, radio, and television, reflect of contemporary culture. Here the connection is far from obvious, for in much of it there is an offbeat note that fails to reflect, even if it does not directly contradict, Christian insights and feelings. However much the work of T. S. Eliot or C. S. Lewis must be appreciated for interpreting Christian truth through literary media, it is not so easy to find an authentic portrayal of religion in the dramas of Tennessee Williams, the essays of Albert Camus, or even in the much lauded *Dr. Zhivago* of Boris Pasternak.[6] What these men do in a searching, even searing, way is to throw a searchlight on life—life and human nature with all its shadows and occasional gleams of brightness.

This is not religion. But it is the portrayal of the human predicament—that to which religion must speak. It is the portraiture of that to which the Christian gospel must speak if it is true to its mission and our Lord's example. To speak only to those already convinced is never enough. If not only ministers but also discerning laymen can find in contemporary literature and drama the signs of the times and the beating of human hearts, such a stethoscope can serve a useful purpose in the kingdom of God.

[6] See "The Sickness of an Affluent Society," Robert E. Fitch, *Religion in Life,* XXIX, No. 4 (Autumn, 1960), pp. 608-14. He contends that both *J. B.* and *Dr. Zhivago* reflect the luxury of self-pity.

5. TO WHAT END?

This chapter has attempted to give a glimpse of some newer movements in the American scene whereby laymen are emerging from the status of "second-class Christians" and seeing the possibilities of a deeper and broader service. Apologies are offered to the numerous centers and movements which there has been no space to describe. Those included are illustrative of types.

What comes of all this? Does it really make a difference? I know of no project mentioned that is one hundred per cent successful. There are barriers in the way, including not only human ignorance and lack of skills, but also human jealousies and lethargies, and as a result slender financial support and sometimes slender acceptance of the possibilities that are open.

Yet, on the whole, such undertakings as have been described have in a few years accomplished much. More can be expected as information is spread and momentum gathered. Dependable accounts are given of increased financial contributions to churches; of acceptance of new responsibilities in local congregations; of disciplines of study and prayer; of acceptance by laymen of calls to missionary service; of new adventures in the arts; of dedication of personal talents, whether full-time, leisure time, or retired time, to various church-related forms of Christian service. Since much of what has come about is in the reordering of inner attitudes and motives, only God can know all.

This is much, but it is not enough. What is needed further is an extension of the layman's stewardship and sense of mission to the whole of life, the meeting of the laity's God-given obligation to be the Church within the world.

Chapter IX

THE CALL TO UNITY

WE CONCLUDE THIS BOOK WITH A BRIEF LOOK AT A LARGE ISSUE, the need for unity within our churches, and through the churches for greater unity within our world. In a sense the whole book has dealt with this theme from various angles, descriptive and historical, theoretical and practical. It is appropriate that we pull together some of these threads in a concluding postscript.

Our world today is torn apart with dissensions of which international strife and the cold war, the tensions in lands emerging from colonialism to nationhood, racial strife that is almost world-wide in its subtler forms and overt in many places, labor and management disputes and much else, are large-scale evidences of a deep uneasiness in our society. At the same time, the drive toward conformity goes on unabated. However much we may speak glibly of individualism within a free society, the pressures on "the organization man" continue to mold us; the "hidden persuaders" seek to make up our minds for us.

We have noted how these forces, both toward dissension and toward conformity, have made their impact on the churches to stifle prophetic speaking and acting and to mold the churches in the direction of safe and sane, respectable social institutions. We have also noted on the other side of the ledger some vital things that churches not only could do but actually are doing to combat both dissension and conformity with "the sword of the Spirit," the power of the Christian gospel.

If the Church of today is to do these things and others yet to be devised with creative fidelity to its gospel, it must set its own house in order. The call to unity is unequivocal. At three levels this is also a call to stewardship or to mission and is bound together with it. At none of these does unity call for uniformity or the blotting out of differences of opinion, patterns of action, or functions in service. At all of them a better understanding, a closer fellowship, and a more unified effort are imperative.

The first of these is at the ecumenical level. As was stressed in the early chapters of this book, the Church Universal which is the Body of Christ ought not to be as divided as it is. Yet the existence of denominations is not in itself a sin against God. It is, rather, an evidence of the rich variety of thought and practice which has emerged under historical conditions through what for the most part has been conscientiously held conviction. No one could truly claim that there has never been any personal or group ambition or collective stupidity in the schisms which have brought denominations into being; yet at least with reference to the major ones this has not been their dominant source. Furthermore, there is no prospect that in the foreseeable future all Protestantism will reunite to form a structure as monolithic as the Roman Catholic Church, even if it were thought to be desirable.

Yet this is not the whole story. If the sundered Body of Christ is to be reunited and the world served thereby, it is Christian unity, not organic union, that will do it. Christians of many denominations including not only the Eastern Orthodox as at present, but also the Roman Catholic, must learn to live together, talk together in fellowship, work together for the service of the world, and upon appropriate occasions, worship together in a common loyalty to Christ for the glory of God. This last need, which from one angle is the most important, is from the standpoint of the Lord's Supper the most difficult. Differences here stem from deep conviction, and intercommunion cannot be rushed. Members of the free churches who do not feel these scruples and are prone to champ with impatience at the reluctance of some fellow Christians to have full and open communion with them had better realize this fact. Yet, fortunately, Christian unity need not wait for either organic union or intercommunion to be achieved.

"Doctrine divides but service unites," so said the late Archbishop Nathan Söderblom of Sweden, one of the chief progenitors of the Life and Work movement which merged with Faith and Order to become the World Council of Churches. This statement is oversimplified if it is quoted, as has too often been done, to suggest that doctrine does not really matter. It matters greatly, not only in the great consensus of Christian agreement regarding God, Christ, and the Holy Spirit but in regard to that area of doctrine where, as we have noted, the disagreement is sharpest—the nature and authority of the Church and its sacramental ministry. Nevertheless, if the quotation is not pushed beyond what the Archbishop intended it is profoundly true. It is in working together for the service of the world—that is, for the increase of the love of God and neighbor—that differences recede, bonds of fellowship are knit, and human good is done.

The second area of unity is that which has been central in this book, the common ministry of clergy and laity. I hope it has been made clear that there are differences of function within this common ministry and that I do not ask the laity to administer the sacraments or do much of the preaching from the pulpit. "Layman's Sunday" when the layman turns preacher is often a rather dismal affair, and since *every* Sunday ought to be layman's Sunday I am not enthusiastic about the idea. Yet if the thesis of this book has been sound, there are great common elements of ministry in worship, fellowship, education, counsel, stewardship, and mission for the clergy and laity to do together. Furthermore, there is "a world of things to be done" to serve the world of today. The thirty-five areas listed and the three especially discussed in Chapter VI are just a suggestion of them. In these basic and far-reaching social problems it is the laity who are closest to them. If the laity fail at these points, regardless of the finest of statements by church assemblies of distinguished churchmen, then the Church fails.

Can Christian laymen by themselves, or by themselves with the help of the clergy, accomplish these things so greatly needing to be done? The answer is No. They can do a great deal, enough to turn the tide from despair to hope and make the solution of even the gravest of these problems an active possibility. But more is needed. What more?

The obvious answer is the power and strength of God. Without the leading and strength that comes from the Source of all being, the best efforts will flounder and may head toward failure. On the other hand, the word of Gamaliel in a time of tension still rings true, "If it is of God, you will not be able to overthrow them" (Acts 5:39).

Yet God requires human helpers. Some of these are His devoted servants, to whom this book is mainly addressed. Some are indifferent to Him; some even flout Him and scoff at His name. God moves in the human scene through the constructive effort of Christians, of religious persons of other faiths, and of some who profess no religion. This is by no means to say that all are equally open channels or that all motivations are equally good. It is only to say that Christians have no exclusive rights in the terrain of good deeds by which the world is served and the kingdom of God advanced.

If this be true, we are brought to the third kind of unity, the need for Christians, both laity and clergy, to work with men of good will outside the Christian faith for the service of the world. To glance again at our list of thirty-five major problems, which of them can be brought to satisfactory solution by Christians only? All of them require the co-operative effort of many Americans and most of them, particularly in the field of world peace, require the co-operation of many nations. These nations, to say nothing of the American scene, include persons of deep adherence to other religious faiths, persons of no religious faith, and persons who scoff at all religion but who still desire the peace of the world. To work with such persons with patience, persistent courage, and such fellowship as is possible is not easy, but it is imperative.

Christians ought at all times to work from Christian motives, letting their understanding of what God requires for the doing of His will in the human scene determine their ends and the general tenor of their means. Some of these ends will be shared by others who feel no Christian conviction or imperative. Many of the means are matters of technical skill and competence, in which there is no special Christian directive except to do the best job possible under the circumstances. Although both in the shaping of ends and the choosing of means Christians must work with those not of the household of faith, the Christian ought never to lose sight of his ultimate goals. As he presses toward them, some forms of co-operation will be easy, others difficult, others impossible. Compromise in the form of adjustment both to circumstances and to the wills of others may be needed at many points, but where compromise calls for the violation of deep conviction, there it must stop.

It often happens that such co-operation is not easy, precipitating harsh words and unkind epithets, if not more serious consequences; endangering both personal safety and that of others; and often ending temporarily in stalemate for one's cause and in what looks like defeat. Because of these factors we are inclined—whether as clergy or lay Christians—to give up in despair and withdraw to more comfortable areas of living and serving. There is, of course, need of reasoned calculation as to where one's effort will be most fruitful. Yet what is needed most is the courage and fidelity of the cross to keep on serving and trusting even in the midst of apparent defeat. It lies at the heart of our faith that beyond the Cross lies the Resurrection morning when God's victory turns defeat to triumph.

So, let no Christian whether clergyman or layman think lightly of his calling! Let none "grow weary in well-doing," for the biblical promise still holds that in due season we shall reap if we do not lose heart. It is through a fidelity born of trust in the power of God and the Lordship of Christ that the Church has survived many crises in the past and has come to the present day of challenge and opportunity. It is through such trust and such fidelity on the part of both its clergy and its laity that it will go forward in its ministry to the world.

SELECTED BIBLIOGRAPHY

A. *The Nature of the Church*

Many books have been written on this theme. Among the most useful are the following:

Brown, Robert McAfee. *The Significance of the Church.* Philadelphia: The Westminster Press, 1956.

———. *The Spirit of Protestantism.* New York: Oxford University Press, 1961.

Herberg, Will. *Protestant, Catholic, Jew.* Garden City, N.Y.: Doubleday & Company, Inc., 1955.

Jenkins, Daniel. *The Strangeness of the Church.* Garden City, N.Y.: Doubleday & Company, Inc., 1955.

Knox, John. *The Early Church and the Coming Great Church.* Nashville: Abingdon Press, 1955.

Lee, Robert. *The Social Sources of Church Unity.* Nashville: Abingdon Press, 1960.

Marty, Martin E. *The New Shape of American Religion.* New York: Harper & Brothers, 1959.

Newbigin, Lesslie. *The Household of God.* New York: Friendship Press, 1954.

Niebuhr, H. Richard. *The Social Sources of Denominationalism.* New York: Henry Holt & Company, Inc., 1929.

Pelikan, Jaroslav. *The Riddle of Roman Catholicism.* Nashville: Abingdon Press, 1959.

Welch, Claude. *The Reality of the Church.* New York: Charles Scribner's Sons, 1958.

Also the following books prepared in connection with major ecumenical conferences:

Evanston Speaks, section 1, "Our Oneness in Christ and Our Disunity as Churches." Geneva and New York: World Council of Churches, 1954. The Evanston report.

Flew, R. Newton (ed.). *The Nature of the Church.* New York: Harper & Brothers, 1952. The Lund preparatory study.

Minear, Paul S. (ed.). *The Nature of the Unity We Seek.* St. Louis: The Bethany Press, 1958. The Oberlin report.

The Universal Church in God's Design. (*Man's Disorder and God's Design,* Vol. I.) New York: Harper & Brothers, 1948. The Amsterdam Series.

The Church and Its Laity

B. *Ecclesiology of the Laity*

Little has been published on this theme. However, the following are helpful treatments:

Come, Arnold B. *Agents of Reconciliation.* Philadelphia: The Westminster Press, 1960.

Congar, Fr. Yves M. J. *Lay People in the Church.* Translated by Donald Attwater. Westminster, Md.: Newman Press, 1951, 1957. A Roman Catholic view.

Evanston Speaks, section 6, "The Laity—The Christian in His Vocation." Geneva and New York: World Council of Churches, 1954. The Evanston report.

Kraemer, Hendrik. *A Theology of the Laity.* Philadelphia: The Westminster Press, 1958.

Robinson, William. *Completing the Reformation.* Lexington, Ky.: College of the Bible, 1955.

Current issues of *Laity,* published by the Department on the Laity of the World Council of Churches.

C. *Work and Vocation*

It is in this area that most of the writing in regard to laymen has been done.

Calhoun, Robert L. *God and the Common Life.* Hamden, Conn.: Shoe String Press, 1954; New York: Association Press, 1957.

Forrester, W. R. *Christian Vocation.* New York: Charles Scribner's Sons, 1953.

Frakes, Margaret. *Bridges to Understanding.* Philadelphia: Muhlenberg Press, 1960.

MacLeod, George F. *Only One Way Left.* Glasgow: The Iona Community, 1956.

Miller, Alexander. *Christian Faith and My Job.* New York: Association Press, 1946.

Nelson, John Oliver (ed.). *Work and Vocation.* New York: Harper & Brothers, 1954.

Trueblood, D. Elton. *Your Other Vocation.* New York: Harper & Brothers, 1952.

Wingren, Gustav. *Luther on Vocation.* Translated by Carl C. Rasmussen. Philadelphia: Muhlenberg Press, 1957.

See also the publications of the Department of the Church and Economic Life of the National Council of Churches, 475 Riverside Drive, New York 27, N.Y.

INDEX

INDEX